THE SKY IS MY HOME

Also by Pamela Bauer Mueller

The Kiska Trilogy
The Bumpedy Road
Rain City Cats
Eight Paws to Georgia

Hello, Goodbye, I Love You
Aloha Crossing

Historical Novels
Neptune's Honor
An Angry Drum Echoed
Splendid Isolation
Water To My Soul
Lady Unveiled
A Shadow of Hope
Fly, Fly Away

The Sky
is my
Home

The Story of Hazel Jane Raines

Pamela Bauer Mueller

PIÑATA PUBLISHING

Piñata Publishing
626 Old Plantation Road
Jekyll Island, GA 31527
(912) 635-9402
www.pinatapub.com

Library of Congress Control Number: 2022931365
ISBN 978-0-9809163-7-9

Cover art by Gini Steele

Typeset by Vancouver Desktop Publishing Centre

Printed and bound in the United States by Cushing-Malloy Books.

*I dedicate this book to my mother, Phyllis Bauer,
who would have loved knowing Hazel Raines.
You will read my newest book in Heaven, where
you are singing and dancing with our Lord.
Thank you, Mama.
You will always be my shining light.*

"But can we afford to deny women work?"

—*Eleanor Roosevelt, September 1, 1942*

"Strength and dignity are her clothing,
And she smiles at the future."

—*Proverbs 31:25*

AUTHOR'S NOTE

Undertaking a new book has always been an extreme challenge. These last two years of research and writing were especially difficult. I lost my mother in March: she was 100 years old. Six months later Mike and I lost our beloved cat, Morgan Maurice. The Covid pandemic ravaged our country and the world, keeping us homebound on Jekyll Island. I realized the time had come to find a new subject and write. I chose Hazel Jane Raines—the first woman in Georgia to get her aviator's license.

Those of you who have read my previous books know how important historical research is to me, and that I usually visit where my protagonist had lived and traveled. Hazel Raines was from Macon, Georgia, so I could see her homes, schools, church, and community. But I could not follow her through Europe, or see where she taught Brazilian pilots in San Paulo. I would have gladly traveled there if the Covid pandemic hadn't stopped me.

Having discovered Hazel's very satisfying voice through her letters, I felt that many of her ambitions mirrored my own.

I wrote this book as if constructing a building. First the foundation and structural skeleton (the plot). Then came the details giving it depth and description: how Hazel started out, what had motivated her, and where her travels would end. This felt like an automobile journey to a place

I'd never been. I had enough details about where Hazel and I would travel along the way, but the specifics of the adventures remained a surprise.

This story mixes real people and events with several fictional people and incidents. This is a new approach for me in writing historical novels. For all my other historical novels, I've found enough sources to concentrate on real people and events. Here, I had only Hazel's family's information taken from letters she wrote to them, and needed to expand on it.

I continued my research into diaries, speeches, and newspaper accounts. I formed my own understanding of her desires, motivations and struggles. I wanted to remain true to the historical narrative of Hazel's life. Her voice and internal dialogues are based on my own interpretations.

A few minor players are fictional. All of the letters are genuine. Her experiences as a pilot are authentic. I created several events in Hazel's life, grafting fiction onto truth in order to reach a wider audience so that people could understand this tumultuous period of time, and Hazel's amazing contributions.

I hope her story inspires you.

ACKNOWLEDGMENTS

First and foremost, I offer my deepest gratitude to God, who has given me the words to share this story. Thank you for Your amazing Grace, and for never letting go of me.

I am deeply indebted to Mark Abbott Hawkins and his siblings—Jack Milton Hawkins and Frankie Hawkins Hobbs. They are the grown children of Regina Hawkins— author of "*Pioneer Lady of Flight*"—my primary source for Hazel Raines' story. Regina Hawkins was Hazel's older sister, and the great-aunt of Jack, Frankie and Mark. Not only has this family granted me permission to use the letters and photographs in this book, but they also mailed me Hazel's photo album, with over 100 photographs, to be used at my discretion. This very kind gesture was a huge blessing to receive at the end of my writing. Thank you Jack, Frankie and Mark from the bottom of my heart.

A very special thanks to my brilliant editor, Carey "Trip" Giudidi, for bringing this book over some rough patches to its final form. I have been so fortunate to benefit from his editing assistance in each one of my historical novels. His crazy good editorial skills, including merciless cuts, reassurance and encouragement, have brought me comfort, support and clarity every step of the way. Trip has always shown absolute commitment to my work. Thank you, Trip, for your friendship and your talent.

Enormous thanks and appreciation go to Ruthmary

Williams, my good friend and next-door neighbor. During a long walk last year, I confessed that I felt ready to write again, and eager to honor a Georgia woman in my next story. Several days later she gave me a list of ten Georgia women who had inspired many over the past two centuries. I studied them all; Hazel's story touched me the most. Thank you, Ruthmary! I would probably never have found her without you.

Huge thanks to my earliest readers—my proofreaders—who are the best. We've worked together as a team through the last seven novels. You ladies are such an important part of my writing family! Thank you Suzi Hassel, Diane Knight and Cathy Drury for your insightfulness, attention to detail and for asking me all the right questions.

My dear artist friend Gini Steel has provided book cover art since my second historical novel. This is the seventh piece of her art to grace my book covers. Her work is always "perfect," and she seems to understand my concept even before I do! I thank you wholeheartedly for your patience, insight and especially for your friendship.

Patty Osborne, I thank you profoundly for coming out of retirement to work with me once again! Patty is my extremely talented "bookmaker," who has been with me since I wrote my very first children's book: *The Bumpedy Road.* She's a master at transforming Gini's art and my manuscript into beautiful books. Thank you once again for wielding your special magic.

I extend enormous gratitude and admiration to the *Middle Georgia Regional Library* in Macon, Georgia. Their Genealogical Department is amazing, and was so helpful in finding the photos, addresses, newspaper articles, etc. that

I requested. Genealogy Researcher James O'Neal worked closely with my husband and me on the research. The day we visited him, he took as much time as we needed to print out what we requested, and then found addresses for Hazel's home and church. His supervisor, Muriel McDowell Jackson, Head Genealogy Librarian/Archivist, also met with us and answered our many questions. A heartfelt thank you to both of you!

Special thanks go to Dr. Vivian Rogers, Research Center Director at the *National Museum of the Mighty Eighth Air Force Museum* in Savannah, Georgia. Dr. Rogers kindly answered my questions and guided me to the proper sources I requested.

Ms. Shelia Bickle, Manager of the Special Collections Research and Support Services at the *Texas Women's University,* was so helpful in finding me important photographs of Hazel that I needed. Thank you, Shelia, for your assistance.

I want to thank the wonderful readers who communicate with me through emails, Facebook messages, phone calls, and letters. I've met many of you and truly appreciate your excitement when a new book comes out. You keep me writing. Your enthusiasm and kind words mean so much to me.

My husband Michael has always been ready to nudge, cheer me on and carry me as I write. And for the very first time, he helped me write this one! Mike actually wrote most of chapter 11. He has been flying for 20 years, beginning in Canada where he received his pilot's license. Naturally Hazel's story was exciting to him since he can deeply relate to her love of flying. I always "emote" with my protagonists, so I really enjoyed flying with him again and seeing many novel experiences through a different lens.

Thank you, dearest Mike, for your generous spirit, your encouragement and especially your patience. Thanks for cooking dinners and breakfasts when I'm deep into research or writing. You kept the candle burning in the window. Thank you for understanding that writing is a big part of why I'm here. But most importantly, thank you for your strong love.

PROLOGUE

MARCH 2, 1943

This morning, as I climb into the Spitfire at the Hamble Airfield in Hampshire, England, I'm not happy with the weather report. But things change quickly, and I hope it will improve during the flight.

The pre-flight mechanic, who has just waved me off with a cheery "Ta-Ra!" left me the smell of oil and a whiff of disinfectant to remember him by.

Today's assignment is to ferry another Spitfire to a fighter squadron—a task I regularly perform. As always, I meticulously inspect the plane before climbing in. I give my "In God We Trust" silver dollar a rub, put it back in my pocket, and whisper a fast prayer.

I manually prime with the Ki-gas pump, and the supercharged Spit is soon climbing to its minimal altitude, lower than the 20,000 feet it would be cruising if it were intercepting a bomber formation later that day.

My much more leisurely ferry flight gives me time to plan what I'll be writing to Mother this evening.

She and I have been in more frequent contact over the past month, and she seems to understand the intense joy I feel when soaring so high above the earth.

Here's the letter I plan to write her today.

Dearest Mother,

If only you knew how happy I am when I fly. I have never felt so completely close to God as when I'm up in the blue. So if you ever get a message that I've been in a crackup and have been killed, don't grieve for me more than you can possibly help; just know I died the way I wanted to.

Flying is, for me, an incurable disease. I need to stay positive now to reassure my family that I'm doing exactly what I want. The words to one of my favorite hymns—"When We All Get to Heaven"—pop into my mind, and I sing out loud and off-key to the Heavens above.

About halfway to my destination, the weather becomes frightful and starts to close in around me. A strange mist makes me feel displaced in time and space, as if I'm flying through some primordial world. I shake my head and try to relax.

And then, the plane cuts out on me. It simply refuses to run any longer! I try re-starting the engine...but nothing. I try again.

My magical bird begins to plummet. The training for surviving crashes races through my mind while I struggle to keep calm. Realizing I don't have enough altitude to jump, I know I have to stay with the plane.

Skimming over almost obscured ground too fast to map-read, I keep my eyes on the murky white ground. I am so sure that I'm flying in the right direction that I continue my path forward.

I don't have time to be frightened. Reminding myself that I love a challenge, I nervously jam two sticks of

Wrigley's Double Mint chewing gum in my mouth. I have to concentrate on my landing strategy.

"Dear God, you are my co-pilot," I whisper. "Please keep my mind clear." I'm still guiding my stricken aircraft, gliding through the murk, waiting to break cloud cover. I promise myself to land without tearing up the plane. I have to maintain a safe airspeed and glide path while I find a good landing spot.

How I wish I could talk to someone! But to avoid the Germans, all of us fly without radio contact.

When I fly into a fog bank, I can't see above, below or ahead. "God, I give this to you," I pray out loud, willing myself to stay calm. For a brief moment, I feel something soft caressing my cheek.

I look down and realize the fog bank doesn't reach ground level. I feel an odd kinship with the colors of the earth below. They seem intensified, and I can make out a farmer moving slowly back and forth across his hilly field.

Suddenly, a large thatched roof fills the cockpit glass. I try turning to avoid it, but it is already too close! I lower my head and double over, grabbing my seat. Just then I hear and feel an enormous BOOM! Everything goes black.

ONE

"We are so proud of you, Hazel Jane," Daddy whispers in my ear. His eyes are brimming with tears.

"Thank you, Daddy," I smile, squeezing his hand. "And thanks, Mother. I know it hasn't been easy watching me learn to fly these past few years." She stands up to hug me, dabbing at her eyes with a handkerchief.

Daddy raises their champagne goblets. "Here's to you, Hazel Jane Raines—our beautiful daughter and Georgia's first licensed female pilot!"

Now my own eyes fill. I cough, trying to pull myself together. "I do have all the licenses now, don't I? Let me see, I got my solo license in 1938, my private license in 1939, and this year, my commercial license. And now I can finally participate full-time in the "World Premiere of a Three Ring Air Circus.""

Checking his watch, Daddy reaches into his pants pocket. "Your mother and I want to give you something to always remember this day, and our love." Holding Mother's hand, he offers me a beautifully-wrapped gift—a tiny jewelry box.

I gasp to see a shiny silver dollar, inscribed with the words "In God We Trust."

"This is for you to carry during your future flights, at take-offs, landings, and whenever you need God close to your heart," my mother says. "You know many beautiful prayers, but my favorite has always been the simplest: 'Thank you Lord'. It represents your gratitude for all the blessings God has in store for you."

I'm speechless. I want to say something but my tight throat won't let me. My parents have given me the perfect gift. "I promise to cherish this memory and this beautiful silver coin forever."

"There's some history behind this coin," Daddy explains. "This motto has been on gold and silver dollar coins since July 1, 1908. Your mother and I thought it was just right for you."

I hug them tightly. "It's perfect. I'm so touched by your gift."

"Now it's time to go to your sister's house for the family celebration," my mother reminds us. "We mustn't be late. She has dinner in the oven."

"Thank you both so much, and please know that I was only able to do this thanks to your support and confidence."

My parents, Bessie and Frank, have always been my greatest influences. They found happiness in our family, faith, and their uncomplicated lives. My father gave me his deep blue eyes, light brown hair, tenacity, his sarcastic sense of humor, and his family name—Raines. My mother gave me my freckles, her beautiful teeth, kindness, and confidence in myself.

Even as a child I knew I wanted more than to live a contented life in Macon, Georgia. I remember so vividly the day my father first carried me on his shoulders down to the Ocmulgee River and pretended to lose his balance.

Rather than being terrified of falling into the river, I was thrilled by that sensation of flying. My first time in an airplane gave me the same awareness of freedom and adventure, self-confidence and excitement. From that day on, flying was all I wanted to do.

As my older sisters got married and raised their children, I found work flying around the South in aerial shows. I knew it was time to leave the nest. If I had known then that Daddy would die of a stroke several months later, I would never have left Mother alone so soon.

Having been born with an unspecified heart condition and chronic asthma, I used to say I was made from "extra parts." Because I love challenges, I refused to let these health issues stop me from living the life I wanted. During my last year in Wesleyan College, a school friend bet me $5.00 that I would never become a barnstormer/acrobatic performer. I had to convince my parents to let me take flying lessons (and pay for them with my earnings and savings) at the Herbert Smart Airport near Macon. In just two years, I earned my solo license, and the next year, my private one, and finally, my commercial license. Now I fly as a stunt pilot and have been touring with the *Georgia Air Races and Shows* all around the South.

Although my mother has never felt completely comfortable with my flying, my father soon shared my excitement, and constantly reassured her that I could fly safely. They started a scrapbook of newspaper articles and photos to show their friends. This early article was from *The Cordele Dispatch*, written on April 19, 1940.

One of the most thrilling acts of the show will be an aerobatic flying act by Miss Raines, holder of the highest license of any woman in the South. Hazel, who has been flying for the past four years, is known as one of the most daring pilots to perform acrobatic stunts. In her performance in Cordele Sunday, she will attempt to break her record of straight loops and spins. Hazel says she will try to start looping the plane at about 5,000 feet and continue to loop it on down to 1,500 feet and then start the plane in a mad spin. The ship is out of control at that point, and she must pull it out of the spin at 500 feet. Hazel will also compete against veteran pilots in the races on the program.

Then my first solo flight was recorded in the *Banner Herald* in Athens, Georgia, written on October 22, 1940. I loved the humor of this piece.

Macon Aviatrix Reaches Goal
By Circular Route

Hazel Raines, pretty Macon aviatrix, arrived in time tonight for a banquet preceding a gigantic air show here tomorrow, but she had the time of her life doing it.

Miss Raines hopped off from Macon shortly after 3 o'clock, flying alone toward Athens. It was her first solo flight of any distance, but she set her compass and headed for the classic city.

An extremely strong cross wind that threw several more experienced pilots off their course slightly blew Miss Raines to the north of Athens and started a series of the most thrilling experiences the young lady ever had.

"The first time I realized I was off course was when I came to a small town, dropped down to get my bearings, and saw a big sign reading 'Toccoa Tombstone Company.' I immediately turned south and it wasn't long until the motor of my plane went dead and there was nothing else to do except look for a place to land. There wasn't any emergency field, or at least I couldn't find one, but I did spot a fairly smooth wheat field and glided down on it for the landing. I landed okay and without damaging the ship, only to come face to face with a farmer, about ten kids and a double-barrel shotgun pointed at me.

The farmer wanted to know what I was doing in his wheat field. I said, 'Well, my motor went dead and I had to make a forced landing.' That seemed to satisfy him and he lowered his shotgun, agreed to hitch a mule to his buggy and carry me to Toccoa eight miles away. I got to Toccoa three minutes before the train pulled out to Gainesville, boarded it and after arriving in Gainesville, caught a taxi to Athens."

I could only imagine how my mother felt when she read this!

The first time I flew with an instructor rekindled my love of freedom. The engine started and we taxied out for takeoff. The plane was so small, so close to the grass and fragile looking. At the end of the runway, my instructor sped up the engine, looked around for any landing aircraft, and lined up for takeoff.

We gained speed down the runway and were suddenly airborne. In the quiet late afternoon air, we circled above the streets, the trees, and even above our blue-green shadows on the grass. Then the ground was behind us, and we rose to the sparkling air filled with sunlight.

While learning the stalls, loops, rolls and spins that make up aerobatics, I discovered new ways to achieve the type of fulfillment my Daddy taught me to value. I imagined the airplane as an extension of my body when I soared over the top and into the leisurely start of a stall. I loved finding myself upside down over several thousand feet of air in an open-cockpit plane. And I really loved knowing how much we barnstormers thrill and delight the crowds that watch us!

TWO

I enjoyed my four years at Wesleyan College, where I ultimately majored in music in the school's conservatory. Wesleyan is a liberal arts college, founded a century earlier as the Georgia Female Institute, so I felt right at home with the other women learning self-confidence and searching for a sense of equality. College was especially liberating to me, and I quickly broke away from the expectations of a traditional Southern womanhood. What would I do instead? I really liked studying music, but I knew that would never be my career.

During my third year of studies, I often remembered "flying" on my father's shoulders as a little girl. I was slowly becoming enthralled with the idea of flying. What would it be like to enter what had always been a man's world of aviation? What a swell way to see the world and keep testing my abilities! Some friends and I went to see a barnstorming event and were riveted by the aerobatic stunts. I told them I was thinking of doing that after graduation.

"Do you mean becoming an aviatrix, or an aerobatic flyer?" asked my classmate Ginny in disbelief.

"Hmm, well, I'll probably start with flying lessons at the airport, and then make a decision."

"Hazel Jane, your parents are very conservative and would never approve," my friend Laura declared. "They would make a big deal about your medical issues and the fact that there are almost no female aviators." I couldn't help laughing at the alarmed expressions on my friends' faces.

"Not true! Amelia Earhart is very famous. She flew solo over the Pacific from Honolulu to Oakland, California just last year!"

"She's an exception and she's not Southern," my other classmate Carol argued.

"Your mother would become a mess of nerves if you told her about your idea."

"Carol, what if I told you I'd like to follow in Amelia's footsteps? Could you keep that a secret for the time being?" I asked her. I was as surprised as my friends that I had just reached this momentous decision.

"Only if you agree to a dare," she countered. "I will bet you $5.00 that you won't even finish flying lessons, much less become a barnstormer. Deal?"

I thought for a long moment and stuck out my hand. "Yes, and we have witnesses. How much time are you giving me?"

She giggled as we shook hands. "As much as you need. Up to six years if you want."

Ginny laughed. "Carol, you know that nothing is impossible for Hazel Jane when she makes up her mind. She'll work through all the obstacles, and I predict you'll be paying her $5.00 in about four years."

And that's exactly what happened. I reached both goals and won the bet. I also learned all about Amelia Earhart's Ninety-Niner support group for women in aviation, which I could join after receiving my pilot's license. Like the other members, I proudly united in their mission to help improve the prospects for female pilots.

I was very proud to be a "Georgia peach." I learned that in 1935, after Amelia Earhart's solo flight, Georgia honored her with a grand celebration. The president of Oglethorpe University in Atlanta proclaimed 1935 as the "Year of the Woman." My state had become a national leader in the recognition of women. This helped me convince my parents that my future would be above the clouds.

It wasn't easy to persuade Mother and Daddy that flying was my destiny. After loud arguments and some tears, they finally came to accept how much this meant to me. Seeing my determination and knowing the freedom I felt when airborne, they changed their minds and offered me their complete support. They even helped pay for my flying classes the first year. After that, I was able to pay for most of my lessons by taking a part-time job in a local men's clothing store, where Mother and I bought my flying clothes: short-sleeved shirts, slacks and a good pair of brown leather boots.

Opportunity came knocking shortly after I earned my instructor's rating. One of the Civil Aeronautics Authority examiners, Lt. L.J. Mercure, had written in my performance review: *Hazel Jane Raines' flying is superior to that of the average licensed male pilot.* That recognition of my skills led to my being chosen as one of six women in the U.S. to be certified by the Civilian Pilot Training Program—where I would train pilots for the Army and Navy Air Corps! At this time, the Air Force didn't exist as a separate branch of the Armed Services.

My family was very proud of my new career.

"You will be part of the war effort, Haze," gushed my sister Frankie. "Even if you aren't allowed to fly, you will train those who do!"

The training center was in Cochran, Georgia—not far from home, so I was able to see my mother as well as my sisters Frankie and Martha and their families almost weekly. I loved my nieces and nephews and wanted to be around them. This new job made it possible!

After a few months of training pilots, I interviewed with *The Atlanta Journal* in late July of 1941 and proudly stated that "out of my total of seventeen students, eight have already been accepted into the Navy or Army Air Corps." When people asked me what I did for a living, I smiled and joked that I was a "two-bit flight instructor" for the Civilian Pilot Training Program.

And the fun didn't stop there. I joined the Macon Aero Club, the National Aeronautical Association, and my favorite—the Ninety-Niners, Amelia Earhart's national flight group for women pilots. I also linked up with the "Short Snorters." Members of this unofficial group of American pilots identified themselves with a one dollar bill with the member's name written on it as well as their sponsor's signature. Any time I met another "Short Snorter" and couldn't show this whimsical credential, I had to give them a dollar.

1941 was a turning point in my flying career. I began working at the Thompson School of Aviation in Fort Lauderdale, Florida to train pilots hoping to enlist in the Air Force. Being the only female instructor, everyone treated me like a novelty.

I met and had dinner dates with several single instructors, but friendship was all I wanted. On the other hand, I relished showing off a letter I had received from the U.S. Department of War, hinting that if the U.S. does enter the war in Europe there could be a chance for women flyers to contribute to the war effort, as the English women were already doing.

That was all I needed to know! I now had a new dream, and daily thanked God for my many blessings.

THREE

My sisters and their families were having lunch with our mother in Macon. I missed them so much and arranged to talk to them all on the telephone.

"Did everyone have a good Christmas?" I asked them when my mother answered. "It has been calm and warm down here in Ft. Lauderdale."

The children spoke over each other's voices telling me what they got from Santa Claus, and I laughed at their youthful enthusiasm. Sometimes I wondered if I had made a mistake by moving so far away.

My mother chimed in. "Hazel Jane, now that the U.S. has entered the war in Europe, what will happen to your job?"

Good question. Who knew? We certainly did not but continued conducting smaller classes at the Thompson School of Aviation in Ft. Lauderdale.

I answered her cautiously. "There are rumors they're discontinuing the CPT because of possible invasions on the east and west coasts."

There was a long silence before my sister Martha asked me about a story she had heard.

"Will you be flying to Europe to help ferry the planes?"

"That's also being discussed, but we don't know for sure. There's speculation that Jacqueline Cochran, the

U.S. celebrity pilot, has been asked by President Roosevelt to research a plan for an organization of women pilots to serve with the U.S. Army Air Corps."

"Isn't that swell?" Frankie said as one of my nieces chimed in. "Would you really join them?"

I laughed. "Naturally I would if I could."

Mother cleared her throat. She tried to put on a brave front, but I knew she was worried.

"I've heard that half the military aircraft on Hawaii and most of those in the Philippines were destroyed in the Japanese raids of December 7th. So aircraft and pilots are desperately needed."

"Goodness, Mother. You are really caught up on current events."

"Hazel Jane, did you know that England has been using female pilots since 1939?"

"Yes, Mother, I did. That's common knowledge here in training schools, yet most Americans scoff at it. I do believe we'll be able to help out at some point."

Frankie interrupted again. "But would you go to England and fly over there if you could?"

"I'd love to, Frankie. And here's more good news. Rumor has it that we will be producing many more planes here in the U.S. this year. A co-instructor told me last week that they plan to build 47,000 aircraft in America this year alone! And all these aircraft have to be moved from the factories to their destinations at home and abroad."

Mother was the first to understand where I was going with this. "And you think that they will need female pilots to help move them, right?"

"Yes, I do. Once all civilian male pilots are called up, they will have to allow women to take their places." If only, I thought, crossing my fingers.

"Mother, please don't fret. I have this flying instructor job, and we just learned they are considering employing women as co-pilots in Miami with the Pan American Ferry Company. So you see, I will remain active in aviation one way or another."

I was still teaching my class in early March when I received a telegram from Jacqueline Cochran asking if I would be interested in flying planes in England. *Could you fly to New York Thursday, March 5 for an interview—transportation will be reimbursed; answer Western Union. Jacqueline Cochran!* She was already famous for her aviation speed records and Harman trophies. And she just asked me if I could fly there? YES! Was my dream to work in Europe going to happen after all?

I spent my last eighty-five cents until payday to send a quick reply—*Arrive New York Thursday 6:45 p.m.*

Miss Cochran treated me well that week, paying for all of my expenses. She impressed me as a confident, intelligent woman—one I'd really like to work with.

During our few moments together, she told me about this new opportunity.

"I presented a plan to Robert Lovett, the Secretary of War for Air, recommending that female pilots be mobilized to ferry trainer-type aircraft to air bases. This would free up men for more active roles in the war."

I had already known that Miss Cochran was a determined woman, and that she had made very good connections both in our country and in Britain.

"And this training in England would prepare American female pilots to fly the planes back home, right?"

"Good insight! Indeed it would. And it should work out well since it was President Roosevelt who suggested I approach Mr. Lovett with the idea," she grinned mischievously. I liked her even more now.

She sent me back home to Georgia to wait for orders to go to Dorval Airdrome in Montreal, Quebec, Canada, without even telling me that I'd made the grade.

I found out the next week and eagerly boarded a train for Montreal on March 15, arriving the following day. I took a physical examination, was issued flying togs and assigned a flight instructor. I was just a little concerned about passing the physical exam, with my history of asthma and heart condition, but I passed and moved into Mount Royal Hotel in Montreal. I jokingly tell my new friends here that I was "made out of leftovers" and it has taken twenty-five years to get them to fit properly.

I'm very happy here in Montreal. Another pilot and I spend our mornings on bad weather days out at the Airdrome hangar repair shop. When we aren't flying we are watching and helping the mechanics work on the aircraft. The other girls spend their time flirting with the tall, dark and handsome pilots. Just give me a big shiny aeroplane any day!

We will eventually go to England by ship, sailing from Halifax, Nova Scotia. They say it will take from ten days to three weeks. How I wish we were flying there instead, but I will not complain about it.

The last day of March I am scheduled (weather permitting) to solo a plane that has 550 horsepower, cruises at 185 mph and weighs 4,000 pounds. Our instructors tell us that by the time we get back from England, we'll all be able to fly anything. That excites me more than anything else!

We learned that Jacqueline Cochran had been quoted about the high standards she required for women in our training program. "The women who were chosen were not only highly skilled but also of upstanding character. I did not want to risk failure because of personality problems or the appearance of less than exceptional moral behavior."

Of the forty women chosen by her, fifteen failed to pass the test. Twenty-three were Americans, including Polly Potter, who was already in Britain. She was in the first group and failed the medical exam after arriving, leaving twenty-two Americans and two Canadians.

I was in the second group of five female pilots to sail to England. We left from the mouth of the St. Lawrence River in a convoy of ships, and twenty-seven days later, were thrilled to see the white cliffs of Dover. The twenty-two American pilots recruited by Jacqueline Cochran would become the first American women to fly military aircraft.

FOUR

Jackie Cochran was determined to find a way into the war effort. In 1941, she persuaded friends at the top— General Arnold in America and Lord Beaverbrook in England—to let her fly a bomber across the Atlantic. While in England, she called on Lord Beaverbrook, Minister of Aircraft Production, and met with Pauline Gowen, leader of the women ferry pilots in the Air Transport Auxiliary.

Back in the United States the following month, she received an invitation from the White House to discuss the role of women pilots in the war. She met first with Eleanor Roosevelt, and later with General Arnold and General Olds. These generals were already forming the American Ferry Command—soon to become the Air Transport Command. This special unit has two main missions: moving supplies and equipment between the U.S and overseas combat theaters; and ferrying aircraft from American manufacturing plants to where they were needed for training or use in combat.

Two weeks later, Jacqueline was invited to organize a group of licensed female pilots to join the ATA, the British Air Transport Auxiliary. Seven hundred licensed female pilots in America were being considered, yet only about seventy-five had the necessary experience, including three hundred hours or more of flying time. Jacqueline sent telegrams to forty of them, including Hazel Jane Raines.

Returning to London in April of 1942, Jackie Cochran was honored with the British title of "Flight Captain," just before the arrival of the first five American women who joined the Air Transport Association.

I have decided to keep a journal about my time in England. I'm sending some of these excerpts to my family and friends in letters, but mostly, I'm writing them for my eyes only to avoid confusion or misinterpretation.

We female pilots were going to England to do our bit because America—the land of the free and the home of the brave—would not give us a chance to prove our worth in our own country. So we left it to help out where we could.

The U.S. would not give us passports, so we would have to stay for the "one year duration or minimum of six months." We had no letter from the American Consul to see us through. The British knew this too, so a simple letter from the Canadian Ministry stating "To Whom This May Concern, etc." was our only entry document to England.

Our contract from the English Ferry Pool Service specified that we would serve for twelve months or a minimum of six months. *Salary is $150 per week in U.S. currency, exempt from British taxes. Transportation is paid by England as well as return from point of origin, and $10 per day living expenses during transportation period out-bound. On return, a flat $100.00 for expenses. If employed for one year—the pilot will receive $500.00 cash bonus in U.S. currency.*

We stayed in Halifax, Nova Scotia for one week, and then very secretly, were taken out to a boat—a "Lighter." We thought it would take us out to a larger ship for the trans-Atlantic voyage. Imagine our surprise when we realized that this Lighter was IT! We were going to be traveling on a British fruit boat transporting aluminum!

After breakfast the first morning, we found a notice in our tiny cabin from the Captain to join him for a cup of tea at 11:00 a.m. in his quarters.

The tea turned out to be gin and bitters, served by the Captain's valet Tiger. We waited for the Captain to join us.

The door opened with a bang and in he strolled. "Good morning, ladies. I'm Captain Bill. Orders say I'm to take you to Jolly Ol' England and that I will do, long live the King."

Captain Bill was a short, weather-beaten sailor in an oil-stained work shirt and canvas trousers one size too big for him, held up with a rope. His hands were almost as big as his head.

A few gins and bitters later, we were all good friends and ready for anything, come hell or high water, and believe me, they were both on the horizon!

Twenty-seven days on this fruit boat in the high seas of the North Atlantic seemed like an eternity. There were seven of us—five of us bound to England for duty—and a British Consul with his bride Janine. For almost four weeks we would share a salt water bath. This three- thousand nautical mile crossing would be the greatest adventure I'd ever experienced outside an airplane.

The trip was quite eventful. We saw forty or more U-boats on daily patrol off the eastern seaboard, sinking an average of three ships a day.

Three of our group suffered severe seasickness so my friend Helen and I learned how nurses feel. Captain Bill and

Tiger turned out to be born entertainers, being either flirtatious or protective as the mood struck them. Consul Canning and his wife, when we passed them in the cramped quarters, were friendly yet obviously preoccupied.

Upon arrival in England, we went by train to the sumptuous Savoy Hotel in London, where Miss Cochran was waiting to give us a warm welcome and the news that Winston Churchill, a regular guest, had just left. That same afternoon I enjoyed a long soak in a fresh water bath—my first in twenty-seven days. The tub was a junior size swimming pool: three-by-six feet in size, with enough knobs and tabs to keep me busy all evening. The towels were so large they could have been long white robes.

We were guests of "Jackie" Cochran at a welcoming dinner party, attended by very important people such as Major Beasley—U.S.A. Air Corps and past president of Lockheed Aircraft. Captain Leonard Plugg, a Member of Parliament and the developer of the International Broadcasting Company, also joined us. I had a fairly interesting conversation (lasting five minutes or so) with him about our ferrying work in England, and he seemed interested in featuring us on his station. There were other well-known people whose names I can't remember.

The five of us were in the first group of twelve American pilots to join the ATA. By the time we reached England in May of 1942, the major air battles over Britain had been fought and won by the Royal Air Force, but German aircraft still roamed the skies over England. We ferry pilots would be flying without ammunition, transporting the planes to RAF squadrons and back to be repaired in the factories. We were trained at White Waltham, the ATA

Headquarters near London. Much of what we do is considered to be "military service" and cannot be shared.

In a letter to Mother dated May 12, 1942, I shared some recent experiences.

Dearest Mother: We are here in Maidenhead, England. This is a very lovely and beautiful place—the flowers are in bloom and everywhere you see tulips, sweet peas, etc. Never before have I seen trees and grass so green. The people I've met so far are all swell—you would think they came from the South when it comes to hospitality. Tomorrow we leave for a pool (place to stay) for several weeks for ground and flight training, and then we return here to Maidenhead. Please give my love to all those who ask about me. I am doing fine. Don't worry for there is nothing to worry about, really. Remember—I love you. Hazel

FIVE

~~~⌒

Mother was so excited to tell me she had been interviewed for *The Atlanta Journal* newspaper. Here is part of the article written on July 5, 1942.

Macon Girl Ferries War Planes
By Mary M. Holzeclaw

Mrs. F.G. Raines of 212 Riverdale Drive, Macon, Georgia has the distinction of being the first Georgia mother with a daughter in England's Ferry Service. "No one, more than I, appreciates the fact that it is a wonderful thing to have a daughter who is capable of working in our first line of defense. And I don't oppose Hazel's going over, not audibly, as she had her heart so set on it, but it seems to me it would be an unnatural mother who could work up enthusiasm over such an undertaking. Hazel said, 'If you tell me I cannot go, Mother, I'll give up the thought, but it will break my heart." So, you see, I couldn't say 'no,' I just didn't say 'yes'.

Hazel loves to do a hard job well, and this business of being in the Air Transport Auxiliary calls out all the ability a pilot has. She has to move aircraft that is very valuable and thousands of dollars are entrusted to her every time she takes off. Many of these planes have been damaged, having just returned from a bombing expedition over

Germany, and she ferries them back to the factory for repairs.

Sometimes the territory over which she must fly is dangerous because of enemy planes, and ferry pilots fly without benefit of radio beam or any weapons with which they might protect themselves. She is subject to call at any time, and she must know how to pilot all types of aircraft, how to fly them to and from all factories, and 'pools,' (stations anywhere in the British Isles). The slogan of the ATA is: 'Any aircraft, any time, any address.'

There are things she is not allowed to tell us, but it is enough to know she is alive and well, and doing what she wants to do. She carries a silver dollar her father and I gifted her. Just before she takes off, she massages it over the words, 'In God We Trust.'

She believes that if we trust as though everything depends on us, then we will beat the Germans and the Japanese before long. And she's doing her part, don't you think?"

That interview meant as much to me as it did to my mother. In her last letter, she asked about my homesickness. I do get homesick at times, but I'm still glad I'm here. I'm not only flying in different aircraft and learning new things daily, but I'm also meeting people from all over the world. I'm seeing the British Isles from the air, which very few people can do. I love appreciating the beauty of this country from the skies. Never did I dream I would be flying such aircraft! It is lots of fun and at the same time, it's quite safe. Our instructors really make sure of our ability before they let us take off in a new machine. As for other dangers that my family and friends fret about, it's as quiet and peaceful here as it would be one hundred miles from the nearest human being.

My only problem seems to be my health, but even the doctor says I'm the picture of fitness who happens to have a "fast-beating ticker." My weight is good: I'm down to 135 now (was 159 when I left the U.S.). My asthma bothers me on rainy or cold days, but I don't tell my family so they won't worry, since there is nothing they can do. My medium height makes it challenging to reach the rudder pedals, but I've devised a way to lengthen my legs with wood blocks that fit over the foot pedals. It takes a lot of leg strength to operate these pedals; fortunately, my legs have always been strong.

The best news I have received I've already written in my letters to everyone. We just finished our primary training and received our wings! I have been promoted to Third Officer, and we'll get three days' leave before beginning our Class II Technical and Conversion course. I will move to another pool for these new classes. In two to three weeks, we'll be ferrying Hurricanes and Spitfires for about four months—and then back to school and checked out on twin engine equipment. Exciting!

The lady I am living with is knitting me some thick socks, as well as a blue wool jumper (sweater) to wear under my uniform tunic. It's cold here most of the time, even in June!

I miss fresh veggies and different types of meat. I'm not on rationing and am not hungry, but I long for certain American foods and drink. I don't like drinking tea four times a day, so I usually ask for water. Yesterday we found an American restaurant here in London, and ate honest-to-goodness hamburgers with onions and Cokes! That was the first Coca-Cola I've had since we left Montreal, and it tasted wonderful. Wow!

My sister Frankie sent me a newspaper clipping from *The Atlanta Journal* (June 18, 1942) that was originally printed in London and reprinted in Atlanta, with an added caption about me. I was pleased to see that it contained correct information about our mission.

MACON GIRL FLOUTS DEATH TO FERRY RAF PLANES
Miss Hazel Raines One of Pilots
Who Makes Giant Air Raids Possible
By Kathleen Harriman

Behind the recent 1,000 plane Royal Air Force raids on Germany, and the smaller scale attacks which resumed Wednesday after a two-week layoff because of weather, are the pilots of the British ferry service. They are the ones who make possible the RAF performances that have astonished the democratic world, raising the hopes of the war-weary world that the final scene—Germany's defeat—grows even nearer.

The ferry pilots' work is to return the bombers—unlucky enough to have been caught in the great searchlight belt over Germany—for reconditioning.

I watched the ATA Pool No. 1 pilots, who moved hurriedly to and fro through the long corridors of headquarters, checking in—checking out—always on the move. The mechanics of the ATA are bewildering enough to any civilian. Commodore D'Erlanger, the man who organized the service when the war broke out, tells me that Britain's ATA is larger than all the U.S. commercial air lines together.

I also met Jacqueline Cochran, the American aviatrix who organized the American women's branch of the ATA. "Three hundred ladies right off the bat," Captain Cochran told me. "From those three hundred, I hand-picked ninety-five. Twelve of those are already here. I will introduce them to you. I think I've got a good bunch of girls."

These ladies were a smartly turned out lot. Some wore navy slacks, others the skirt adaptation of the ATA uniform. Each one had ATA wings on her jacket. There was Miss Louise Schurman, daughter of the Counselor General of the Dutch East Indies, now a resident of New York City; Miss Virginia Farr, West Orange, N.J.; Miss S. Ford, New York City; Miss Dorothy Furey, New Orleans; Miss Virginia Garst, Kansas City; Mrs. H. Harrison, Toronto, Ont.; Miss W. Pierce, Mineola, N.Y.; Miss P. Potter, Portland, Ore.; Miss Hazel Raines, Macon, Ga.; Miss Helen Richey, Pittsburg, Pa.; Miss G. Stevenson, Tulsa, Okla; and Miss A. Wood, Waldoboro, Me.

The twelve of us have become good friends. Jackie Cochran is staying here with us and treats us like her children. She's invited my roommate Sue and me to London to have dinner with her Monday night and then spend our day off with her on Tuesday. She's really a lovely person. I've invited her to spend a few days with me when I get back to good old Georgia, and she said she would love that. She even promised me an excellent job in aviation in the States when I return.

SIX

It's the end of August and I am stationed here at White Waltham for Class II Conversion. This quaint village, a few miles west of Maidenhead in Berkshire, is dominated by the airfield with easy access to the continent. I'm still ferrying light equipment such as Masters, Hurricanes, and Spits but hope to make Twins in a couple of months. This week I was promoted from Third Officer to Second Officer: another stripe on my shoulder and an added responsibility to fly faster equipment.

Tonight I'm in Dumfries, Scotland—the sweetest, most interesting little village. Another American girl is here spending the night with me. After dinner, while it was still daylight, we went on a walk and visited the home of the Scottish poet, Robert Burns. After seeing his home, we walked down the cobblestone street to St. Michael's Church, where he is buried.

Burns, who died at age thirty-seven, is still revered by Scots as their national poet. We were so surprised to learn that thirty-seven years after his funeral, a phrenologist robbed his skull from the mausoleum, believing it would unlock the secrets of the poet's genius. I love these fragments of historical education I stumble across here in Scotland.

Well, I bought a motorcycle to resolve the problem of transportation. I got a good second-hand one for about

$150.00. Actually, Grace Stevenson and I bought it together and rode it to London on Sunday. We were a sight rolling through London—me in the back holding on to Grace with one hand and a big suitcase in the other. It was horrid—far worse than riding a horse—so we decided to save and buy a side car.

I wrote to my mother about the motorcycle and without my even asking, she sent me some money for the side car. I also confessed to her that my sisters send me cigarettes, which I smoke infrequently. I needed to get that off my chest, and in her following letter, she sent some money for cigarettes. And, she sent American cheese, our favorite chocolates, and a ham, which was a delightful surprise! My mother is the most wonderful and caring person I know, and I have told her so. What I didn't tell her yet is that a bad cold has settled in my chest and the Station Doctor sent me away for a couple of weeks' rest. He told me I had been working too hard and needed to spend time sleeping and resting in bed. I argued, but he won.

When we first arrived here we met Wing Commander Sidney Cotton, a lifelong aviator who is well-known as an Australian inventor, photographer and aviation and photography pioneer. This man is responsible for developing and promoting an early color film process. He also owns a beautiful apartment in London that overlooks the city, and offered it to us as our headquarters when we are sick or need a place to stay in London. We'd never taken him up on his generous offer before. But here I am, temporarily residing in this lovely place.

Commander Cotton also has a big estate near Maidenhead on the Thames, and he's staying there now while I'm recuperating. Another American pilot, Virginia Garst from Kansas City, is here with me. She's recovering after having her appendix removed almost two weeks ago. Now that we are much better, we've decided to visit his estate and enjoy the sunshine and open air. I'm grateful for the rest and feel a bit like royalty here, yet look forward to returning to work and my conversion course to twin equipment. I'll need all the energy and strength possible.

In another letter to Mother, I asked her how my niece Jeaneane was doing in school. I wrote: *I know she is going to be smart as a whip and truly whiz through her studies—I know Martha will never have to make her study like you had to keep after me. Those must have been awful days for you when I was "just getting by" in school. Sometimes when I think about those days, I just don't see how you had the patience you had with me. I really wasn't dumb, but just didn't like what I was doing. You must be so relieved to know that I've finally found what I love.*

I occasionally wonder if I should reconsider serving the full eighteen months in the ATA. The cold winter weather, recurrent asthma and the tough work occasionally make me long to be back in warm Georgia. And the newly organized American Ferry Command might mean I could keep flying when I return. I will try to make it through this next winter with the help of cold shots, ultra-violet ray treatments and a positive attitude.

Time flies and I've just realized that I've been flying for five years in January! It's meant a lot of work and worry, but I know it's worth it. Now and again I feel sad, especially when asthma kicks in, or the old heart business starts—all of which can be taken care of by bed rest. But I miss the comfort of family, my mother's warm embrace, and playing with my nieces and nephews. I came to Britain for twelve months of service but with an option to serve longer. I might just make it a year and return in April or May. It will depend on how I am physically. I'm due for another promotion as soon as they have room for me in a conversion course.

I wonder if I'm turning into an old maid whose life consists of an eight-hour work day, twelve hours sleep, and an occasional quiet evening at the movies. I've had to resign myself to a sane and simple life of doing nothing but a few hours of flying each day, then spending the rest of it waiting for old age to creep up on me.

SEVEN

On September 1, 1942, First Lady Eleanor Roosevelt showed her support for our team, writing in her daily newspaper column about her constant concern for the American female pilots.

> There is just a chance that this is not a time when women should be patient. We are in a war and we need to fight it with all our ability and every weapon possible. Women pilots, in this particular case, are a weapon waiting to be used.

On the 26th of October, Mrs. Roosevelt came to visit England, very publicly appearing at the Air Transport Auxiliary in White Waltham to show her support for the female pilots.

Winston Churchill's wife accompanied her on a tour of inspection of the Aerodrome. The tour was led by Pauline Gower, the British aviatrix who had founded and run the women's section of the ATA since 1939. We met her once before and were so pleased that she thoughtfully included us in this tour.

The weather was appalling—a typical English October day—and we were dressed in uniform. The various aeroplanes that we had been flying were lined up outside. Standing in the dreadful rain, we held our breath as Mrs. Roosevelt walked by, stopping to meet each one of us.

I was somewhat nervous when she approached me, but she immediately put me at ease. "Where are you from, Miss Raines?" she asked smiling.

"I am from Macon, Georgia, Mrs. Roosevelt, near Warm Springs."

She broke into a big grin. "Oh yes, how well I know where that is!"

I knew her husband had been coming to Warm Springs for many years, exercising in the hot pools as he tried to rebuild his leg muscles from the debilitating effects of polio.

Trying to prolong our conversation, I asked her when he might return.

She laughed softly. "I believe he may even be there now, enjoying our 'Little White House.' He uses it as his retreat from the rigors of leading the nation."

She moved on. In a few moments, we all retired to the Officers' Mess, where we shared a cup of tea with her, Mrs. Churchill and Mrs. Hobby, head of the newly organized WAAC, the Women's Army Auxiliary Corps. As luck would have it, I was seated directly across from Mrs. Roosevelt.

"Are you homesick being so far away from your family?" she asked me.

I wanted to be honest. "Yes, Mrs. Roosevelt. Sometime I am, but I'm so happy to be here doing my small part for the war."

"How do your parents feel about your participation?" she wondered.

"My father has passed, but my mother and sisters cheer me on and approve."

She nodded. "I am quite pleased with your team's work over here, and I feel sure that the U.S. will soon find a role for you. I believe that female pilots are the weapon waiting to be used."

Those words gave me hope and a great appreciation for Mrs. Roosevelt, her friendliness and her interest in helping others.

We then assembled in the hangar where she was introduced by the Minister of Aircraft Production, Col. John Llewellyn. She spoke about the importance of working together for the benefit of all. We had been told to wear skirts for this occasion, so we were completely unprepared for the rain. Without adequate covering, we stood in the rain for half an hour and almost froze to death.

"Did you know that First Lady Eleanor knows Jackie Cochran?" whispered Virginia.

"No. How do you know?" I whispered back.

"Jackie told me. When she won the Harmon Trophy as the World's Outstanding Woman Pilot of the Year in 1939, Eleanor Roosevelt presented her the trophy! In Washington D.C."

It was a very fine day for us—the American female pilots—and I'm certain also for the British contingency.

It's interesting to note something I saw later in the press (*The Telegraph*). It reported that Mrs. Roosevelt was making a speech when we had an air raid. Well, that simply is not true. She had finished her speech, we all said goodbye and she had left the Aerodrome when the alert sounded. I won't forget this for more than one reason— the first being we all had our skirts, shoes and stockings on and we had to go down to this air raid shelter that was ankle deep in water. It was almost comical. There we stood for about thirty minutes, freezing and puddling around in the dark in all the muck and water, checking to make sure all the American girls were accounted for. Then we sang songs at the top of our lungs until it was all over. The second reason I won't forget this is because now we can reassure our loved ones that we don't work all the time. We do take time out for a little fun and song once in a while, even when it's forced on us.

It is November and I've been transferred to another "pool" for three weeks. Presently I'm living in a very old English home (really an estate) that belongs to Lindsay and Lady Everard. The home dates from the early sixteenth century on the site of a Roman villa and Norman manor. There are more than forty rooms here, with enormous fireplaces, a huge ballroom for dancing, another large room for games, and one soundproof room for playing squash. I love the English air of formality this estate carries. Oh, and the Aerodrome where we now study was the Everards' private Aerodrome before the war began.

The garages here accommodate twenty-five automobiles and are packed with cars stored for the duration. Above the garages are twenty small, beautifully furnished rooms with lavatories and steam heating. And this is where two other pilots and I now live! The stables are only about five hundred yards away and have only eight horses at this time, which we enjoy visiting. We have both maid and butler service, and all meals are served with pomp and ceremony. I have to admit I am totally enjoying this and would love to stay here for the rest of my time in England, but I know this just isn't possible.

My earlier Second Officer classes had focused on flying fighter-type aircraft—usually single-seaters ranging from 800 to 2,000 horsepower. Our written examinations covered such subjects as aircraft instruments, propellers, aircraft construction, different engine types, fuel systems, super-chargers, boost control, mixture control and carburetors. I must have studied harder here than any time at school in Georgia. But I really enjoy these courses.

I put in four hours in the Harvard (A-T-6) and then went on to the single-seater fighters. I will never forget my first flight in this machine. And it was impossible to be accompanied by any co-pilot on this flight.

I smiled as I remembered. *There she sat—to me, the largest aeroplane I had ever seen, and as I looked at her from about fifty feet, I slowly walked up and said "Good Morning, Chum." She looked at me and made the most gosh-awful face and seemed to laugh out loud at the tune my knees were playing. I fooled her tho' by getting in and showing her who was boss. After three weeks of circuits and bumps, we were the best of pals and just getting to like each other. That's when they passed me out of the school and back to ferry flight, with a promotion to Second Officer.*

But now I'm back in Maidenhead, and for three weeks I'll get further training on all types of twin engine equipment.

This excites me because after I complete this course, I will have flown practically every type aeroplane that has been built by the United States and Great Britain.

What I'm doing now is truly the realization of a dream I've had since childhood—a dream I had no idea would really come true because it was simply too fantastic. This is the most interesting job I have ever had—breezing along at 250 miles per hour over Scotland, Wales and England. I wonder if anything could be more fun.

EIGHT

I have loved every minute spent flying in and around England, yet there is so much more I could say about the people I've encountered here. They are unfailingly hospitable and friendly. They are more reserved than we Americans, and not as quick to make friends. But after the ice is broken, they are very much like us. Their spirit is so amazing, considering all they have gone through, and their lives seem to be going forward in a sane and normal way.

Each one is doing his or her best to help win the war. There is not an idle hand, no matter how young or old, rich or poor someone may be. There's a job to be done, and these people are doing it. One day they will be rewarded, not through the ultimate victory alone, but through and by the One who holds the fate of all in His all-powerful and justifiable hand.

Extensive bomb damages is being energetically cleared away and made ready for rebuilding. As for air raids, most people take about as much notice of an air raid as a telephone ringing, and go about their daily routines as though nothing were happening. We appreciate and respect these British people, wondering how we would have taken such unrelenting blows and hardships.

It's late November and soon I'll be returning to the "old home pool" in Maidenhead. Before leaving, I want to say how excited I was about my first flight in a different model: a single-seater English fighter. I flew it just after it finished its last raid over Germany. I was pleasantly surprised by how easy it was to handle. It was another thrilling experience for me.

I am very lucky to have found a warm billet for the winter. I'm back with the family I first stayed with: Mr. and Mrs. Roy Littlehales. She was once a famous singer in New York. Her mother, her married daughter and her three-year-old grandchild live with them, because the daughter's husband lives in Egypt. They call me their daughter, and make sure I get milk, good steak and veal and even fresh veggies as often as possible. Mrs. Littlehales pampers me, wrapping my pajamas around my hot water bottle and putting them in my bed just after dinner so they will be warm when I crawl into bed. And her husband greets me at 7:30 every morning with a hot cup of coffee.

I call Mrs. Littlehales "Olga" and just this morning, she showed me a letter she had written to my mother. I was very touched, and I'll share a few lines.

Dear Mrs. Raines,

In the first place, I must tell you that Hazel Jane is very well and full of "Pep". We think she is a lovely girl and just as sweet as well. I know she is happy with us and I am sure you will be glad. I do hope the weather won't be too bad for her. Our climate is rather treacherous. We are going to try to make it a Happy Christmas, but many loved ones will be away.

I hope you will have a Peaceful Christmas. You will miss your Hazel, as she will you. She looks so fine in her uniform and we admire her so much. In fact, my husband

*calls her his second daughter. I think he wants to write a
little here.*

*I think I will butt in to say she is just the sweetest and
swellest girl that the United States could ever send over,
and we are indeed lucky to have her with us. If you should
lose her, you will know we can't part with her. To crown it
all, come over and see us, as we are quite sure such a
grand little woman must have as equally charming
Mother. Au Revoir, and here's to our meeting in happier
times.*

*Please do not worry over your Hazel Jane. I love her
as my own daughter. I will write to you from time to time,
telling you about her.*

*With very best wishes-
Yours very sincerely,
Olga Littlehales*

Shortly after reading this letter, I began to feel worn out and
very tired. The Littlehales insisted I see their family physi-
cian, who sent me to the hospital, where I stayed for two
weeks. Since Christmas was coming, they thought I could
rest, sleep and eat more calmly in the hospital. And during
my stay there, I had quite an experience.

I was sitting up in bed, chatting with three American
girls who were visiting me, when, like a shot out of a shell,
a middle-aged woman came bursting into my room and
said arrogantly, "Where is that gal from Georgia? I want to
see some good old Southern blue blood." I sat up taller
and said: "Here she is—so what?"

Then this moderately-dressed little woman looked intently at me. "Well honey child, I'm from Virginia, and I know all about us folks from the South; and if you are from Georgia, I know I'm talking to a real lady." I saw my friends slipping away from my bed as this visitor continued her conversation. "A real Southern girl would never come off her dignity and do such an unladylike thing as fly a plane."

That set me off. "Well now," I began, "Let me tell you something about flying." And for ten minutes I did just that, ending with "I am of the opinion that the women of today are doing a man's job in a woman's world with unfaultable ability and finesse, and if a woman of your integrity can not see it in that light, she must be a very narrow-minded person indeed."

The lady studied me closely, astonished at my outburst. "Oh my, that's the first time in my life I have ever had anyone speak to me in such a frank manner." She smiled. "However, I like you, Georgia."

I told her it really didn't matter to me whether she liked me or not, since I was merely expressing my feelings. Suddenly, it dawned on me just how rude I had been. My mother would have been appalled.

"Very well then, I should go now but I'll be back tomorrow," she told me, heading toward the door.

I called after her. "Are you a Red Cross worker? Sorry, I didn't get your name."

She smiled pleasantly and replied, "Georgia, everyone calls me Lady Astor."

I laughed caustically at her sense of humor. "Oh really!"

As she turned to go, she repeated, "I'll see you tomorrow."

When the door closed, my friends fell over themselves laughing. Still irritated, I asked them what was so funny.

My friend Sue spoke up. "Well, Hazel Jane, even though you would not believe her, she *is* Lady Astor, and you were extremely disrespectful to her." They recognized her through newspaper photos.

"Dear Lord," I moaned, realizing how terribly I had treated her. "I'll never see her again."

But Lady Astor kept her promise, and the next day returned with Ambassador Phillips, President Roosevelt's personal representative to India, who was leaving for New Delhi. She said my Canadian doctor, Col. Walton, had just given his permission for me to spend the next day at her home.

Before leaving the hospital, a friend told me more about my new friend. Lady Astor had been popular in London's social life even before marrying Lord Astor. As a newcomer to London, she was questioned by an English woman: "Have you come to get our husbands?" Her surprising response was, "If you knew the trouble I had getting rid of mine, you'd never ask."

After her American-born husband Lord Astor succeeded to the peerage and entered the House of Lords, Lady Astor entered politics as a member of the Conservative Party and won her husband's former seat in Plymouth Sutton in 1919. She became the first woman to sit as a Member of Parliament in the House of Commons.

The Astor estate, Cliveden, was one of England's largest and most historical estates. It had been the home to a Prince of Wales, two Dukes, an Earl, and finally the Viscounts Astor. It was also the meeting place of the

Cliveden Set of the 1920s and 30s—a group of political intellectuals.

I had a wonderful time with Lord and Lady Astor, who were lovely to me and acted like they had known me all my life. I have never felt so much at home during a first visit to a new friend's place as I did that day. After tea, Lady Astor told me she had made arrangements with the hospital for my discharge to her care. I would return to Cliveden the following day and spend a week with them during Christmas vacation. That holiday visit cured all of my ailments, and I was healed in body and spirit when I returned to my classes.

NINE

High Flight

OH! I have slipped the surly bonds of earth,
and danced the skies on laughter-silvered
   wings;
Sunward I've climbed and joined the
   tumbling mirth
Of sun split clouds—and done a hundred
   things
You have not dreamed of—wheeled and
   soared and swung—high in the sunlit
   silence.
Hov'ring there, I've chased the shouting
   winds along, and flung my eager craft
   through footless halls of air.

Up, up the long delirious, burning blue, I've
   topped
the windswept heights with easy grace,
Where never lark or eagle flew.
And, while with silent, lifting mind I've trod
   the high un-trespassed sanctity of space,
Put out my hand, and touched the face of
   God.
             —John Gillespie Magee, Jr., 1941

High Flight was written by a nineteen-year-old American pilot who served in the Royal Canadian Air Force in England. His poem had been found in his personal effects in December 1941, just after a fatal crash in which his Spitfire collided with another airplane. Jackie Cochran had given each of her students a copy of this poignant poem. I always carry mine with me when I fly, right next to my silver coin.

After handing out the poem, Jackie told us quietly, "I don't know what led you to accept the challenge and risks of becoming a pilot. Perhaps not all of you are sure, either. By now you know that flying in wartime isn't a Cinderella story. Every flight brings moments of stress and sparks of joy."

She gently furrowed her brow. "Take a moment to think about what led you to choose this career. That might make it easier to share your experiences with your loved ones."

I was in the cockpit just a few hours after she gave us John's poem. I felt a very compelling need to escape into the sky. I wanted to scatter my grief for his loss throughout the clouds, and remember other pilots who were killed in combat. As I cruised, I banked sharply between the floating clouds, brushing the plane's belly along their whipped-cream peaks.

I asked God, "Why him? How do you choose certain people, Lord? I don't understand."

My thoughts grew calmer as I concentrated on the world stretching out all around me. A smile blossomed as I watched the horizon begin to curve. Once I was in the air where I belonged, I searched the sky and playfully dodged the silent white puffs. My engine was humming evenly and the plane answered the pressures on the controls. The light of late afternoon painted the landscape with layers of rare and shimmering gold.

Once again I felt that nothing would go wrong, as long as I could re-discover my sense of peace in my small world.

I was thinking about Jackie's intriguing question and asked myself, *when was the exact moment when I'd first wanted to become a pilot? Was it the first time I barn-stormed?*

Not all of my classmates had been barnstormers; many were curious about my experiences. One wet and windy afternoon, while relaxing together after class, Dorothy asked me about stunts I used to perform.

"Well, I did a lot of things. I dipped and nosedived, roller-coastered, performed lazy eights, flew upside down, looped-the-loop; but my favorite stunt was the high-powered climbing turns called *chandelles*. Those maneuvers were…"

"Did you dance the Charleston in flight, Hazel, since you are a Southerner?" interrupted Helen.

I thought a moment before answering. "No, I didn't, but I saw that one time. The girl was supported only by piano wire as she stood upright on the top wing, while the plane looped-the-loop."

"And what about the audience? I know they were mesmerized and frightened. Did they ask for autographs after the show?"

I laughed, enjoying the memory. "They wanted to, and we'd have been happy to oblige. But we were usually whisked away too fast."

Dorothy jumped back in. "So how did it feel up there?"

I smiled at her question. "Breathtaking. I pulled up into stalls, leaned into steep turns, flipped from one lazy eight to another, and reveled in the easy, light feel of the ship. But you all understand that, right?"

The girls nodded. "Then tell us about the most amazing stunt you ever saw or did." Dorothy was clearly fascinated with the subject, and determined to wring an exciting story out of me.

"Hmm, let's see...I saw a few mid-air changes, where the women climbed up on the wing and executed a plane-to-plane mid-air change. You all know the first rule of wing-walking," I said with a laugh. "Don't let go of the first wing until you've got a good hold on the second!"

After a brief pause to get my thoughts in order, I continued. "Women in the 1920's were the real daredevils. A woman named Phoebe Fairgrave made a record jump from over 15,000 feet in the summer of 1921. Then she developed a double parachute jump, where she cut the first parachute loose to free-fall, before releasing the second. When she was only twenty, she and her husband formed their own flying circus. Today they own a flying school in Memphis called *Mid-South Airways.*"

We learned that many famous pilots like Amelia Earhart and Charles Lindbergh had started out as barnstormers. Yet I was one of only two women in my class who had barnstormed.

"After performing my very first stunt, I knew immediately I'd never stop flying. Flying gets under your skin—deep down inside. You know that. That's why we're here."

As the others fell silent, I asked myself again..."why *am* I here, really?"

I was night-flying and loving it. I would be alone with the stars until dawn crept up from the East. And at dawn, the quietness of the air feels like a caress. There's nothing quite as luxurious as a dawn sky, blossoming with colors and warming us to our core.

But when the noon sun beats down and the skies smile with fluffy clouds, I'm also transported. If I'm flying during the late afternoon, I can't wait for dusk—with the sky drenched in fading light, and nostalgic colors of its own. That's the time of day I often think about brave women pilots who preceded me and opened the doors for us. I remember a quote by Amelia Earhart: "If enough of us keep trying, we'll get someplace."

I wrote to my mother and sisters that flying appeals to me because it takes me somewhere else. It represents independence and free will: a triumph over gravity. Flying is my chance to excel, and to escape from the labyrinth of routine existence. Don't we all need to escape sometimes? To seek the euphoria of freedom? Flying provides both. And, if I should ever perish while flying, I know He will be waiting for me after that final flight.

TEN

Lady Nancy Astor told me that the real reason she had invited me for Christmas was because she wanted her four eligible sons, who were here for the Christmas holiday, to meet a lady from the South, hoping one of them would fall for me. I told her I wasn't ready to fall in love with anyone—not even an Astor. I came to Britain to do a job, and my job had just begun. Her answer surprised me. "It's so unusual to find a young girl who wouldn't jump at the chance to marry someone with money and a name."

Christmas has come and gone. I stayed with the Astors until Christmas Day, then returned to the Littlehales' home—my billet—to spend the rest of the holidays with them, as promised. I knew they had gone all out to get everything perfect so I wouldn't miss my family too much. Olga cooked us a twenty-pound turkey with all the trimmings, and I contributed a fruit cake my mother sent over. I wrote about all this and much more in a letter to my family. Here is just a small portion of that letter.

> *Dearest Mother,*
>
> *It is almost impossible to write you about my visit to Cliveden, so I'll just say they were wonderful to me and I had a lot of fun. On Christmas Eve, I walked all over the*

Estate with the American-born Lord Astor, and he told me some of its history. The original Cliveden was built in 1650 by the Second Duke of Buckingham who, one fine day in 1668, decided to run away with the Countess of Shrewsbury and bring her back to Cliveden. While in the act of escaping they were overtaken by her husband. The two men fought a duel and her husband was killed. The Duke buried the sword he used to kill him, and decorated a section of the grass in his garden with crossed swords and the date 1668. It has continually been cut that way and the date can be seen even today. The original house burned down in 1795; a second was built and torn down when the third was built in 1830. The house now standing is the fourth one, built in 1849 by Sir Charles Barry.

Rather than try to describe the inside of the palace, I have taken pictures and will send them to you. I will tell you that my favorite room is one of the smaller dining rooms, where a fire constantly warms. It was painted a pale peach, and candles burned brightly on the table, adding a rosy glow. One evening just the three of us took our supper there. Cook had made us a fine fish pie, which is very English, as you know. I stuck my nose in the kitchen several times to learn the recipe. It had shrimp, cockles and mussels, strips of haddock, pieces of cod, and bits of onion and celery, all mixed together in a light creamy sauce. This fish casserole was topped by a crust made of thick mashed potatoes, browned in the oven. I know you can just imagine how delicious it was! I will attempt to make it for you on your birthday.

When I get home, we'll have so much to talk about!
Oh, I almost forgot the gloomy part. Lord Astor later
confided to me that the upkeep had become ruinous and
the Estate had long since ceased to provide a family center.
He knew this was the end of an era for Cliveden, which
had been the site of political activities and house parties in
the 1920's and 1930's. He mentioned, with great pride,
"Cliveden was an enchanted kingdom and Nancy was its
queen." Then his eyes transformed and his pained
expression said it all. "So I've offered Cliveden to the
National Trust, which they've happily accepted."

I will never be certain why Nancy Astor was so interested and so kind to me. Perhaps she saw me as the daughter she never had. Or envisioned me as another woman with ambitions like her own. She had undeniably succeeded in a man's world—as Britain's first female Member of Parliament. She also played a prominent role in women's reforms, such as her advocacy for equal opportunity and equal pay. One day she simply said that she loved my sense of humor and perseverance. I still feel humbled by her kindness.

I believe she respected my battle to succeed in the field of aviation by becoming one of the twenty-two women taking part in the British Air Transport Auxiliary in 1942. She understood that many male pilots and military figures were opposed to this plan, even though, by our doing those jobs, we freed up the British pilots for combat duty. All my ambitions—conquering new worlds, meeting interesting people, and living through thrilling adventures—were worlds she had already possessed.

The Astors have invited me back to visit and even arranged to take me to see George Bernard Shaw! They've also invited me to the House of Commons, where I will be able to sit in on a session. I find it so amazing that both are Members of Parliament.

We've had awful weather at the end of December and early January. I have finally seen my first snow storm and didn't like it, even though it was pretty. I was delivering a plane on that day and found myself approaching what I thought were just low clouds. I tried to fly above them but as I climbed, I realized these were not soft fluffy clouds, but rather, a solid mass of snow and hail. I hurriedly turned around and resumed my original route, landing at the nearest Aerodrome just in time! Everyone had a good laugh about my not knowing the difference between snow and clouds, but now I'm becoming an expert.

I'm still ferrying single-engine fighters and will probably continue until spring. I really wanted to transfer to Twins this month, but my commanding officer said he'd prefer I stay on singles a while longer because of my good record. It's true I've not had a crack-up or damaged any equipment as yet (and hope I never do), so I agreed with him. When the time is right, he'll let me know.

My letters to my family are more frequent now since bad weather keeps us grounded for longer periods of time. I miss my family, yet haven't felt motivated to write much. I especially miss my father, who died just after I received my commercial pilot license. My memories of him remain strong, but mostly of my childhood and school years. I've learned that memory is a quantity that gets summoned or evoked; then it's carried to an arena for our viewing pleasure.

Daddy was a successful contractor who took a lot of pride in his work. Every time we drove through Macon, he'd point at a house and say, "That's the Daniels' house I built; they have a beautiful window in the living room," or "The Fulton family who lives there have triplets, so I added a new fence around their yard."

He taught me the importance of good planning. "The most important part of building a good house comes before you pick up a hammer," he'd tell me, even when I was in elementary school. "Every hour you spend designing saves you two or three hours of work later."

Because of him, every time I fly I take a little extra time with the mechanics, making sure every possible surprise has been taken into account. The crew feels appreciated and is eager to do their best for our total effort.

I only wish I had taken Daddy up with me a few times so he could see how much I learned from him. I want to believe he's enjoying my adventures from his heavenly home.

I had a four-day-leave and returned to Maidenhead and the Littlehales' warm house. Olga showed me the sweet, kind letter my mother had written them, and I almost cried while reading it. It's a darn shame it has taken me twenty-six years and three thousand miles of distance to make me realize what a swell mother I have. I will sit down and let her know this right away.

I don't like to worry Mother about raids or black-outs, but my sister Martha asked me about them, so I responded.

> *Dear Martha, in response to your question, let me tell you about the excitement we had the other day. I left to deliver a Spit to an Aerodrome and after landing and getting out of my ship, I looked around for someone to turn the papers over to. I couldn't find a soul. Thinking they had all gone out to tea, I sat down by the plane and waited. Soon I heard the Air Raid Warnings (which must have sent everyone away earlier) but I still sat and waited. Unfortunately, we have become accustomed to them by now and take no notice anymore.*
>
> *The next thing I knew a German plane was spraying machine gun bullets across the field. I jumped up and ran quickly into the surrounding forest. We all knew their aim was not very good, but this plane damaged the equipment they were to use that day and tragically, killed three men. I left as soon as I could. I felt angry and upset. It burns me up that they give us the best fighters built to fly but no ammunition. How I would have liked to take a shot at one of those oppressors!*

Now it's late February, and I've been posted to Southampton. Grace Stevenson and I are living with Mr. and Mrs. G.A. Porter—a couple in their forties. Their lovely home is right on the ocean—only a five-minute walk from the Aerodrome. We are now getting six days off per month, so

I can certainly find time to catch up on letters, mend a few socks, and enjoy some rest.

I've returned to my childhood hobby of gardening radishes. I planted two beds of radishes, but the birds snatched them all up. So, yesterday I replanted and put wire mesh screening over the bed. When Mrs. Porter returned home, I proudly took her outside to see my new effort. The look on her face said it all. Apparently, I had dug out what had been one of her choice flower beds, which I had mistaken for weeds.

Grace and I have invited her to join us at the movies in Southampton this afternoon (to try to make up for my mistake). Then I'll take us all out to dinner. Speaking of dinner, I haven't laid eyes on fried chicken since my last Sunday at home one year ago. During these moments of memories from home, I get really homesick, especially with six days of leave to think about it.

I can't wait for my next flight on March 2nd, when I'll ferry two aircrafts. I'm eager to return to the freedom that exploring the skies always brings me.

ELEVEN

This morning I feel a bit giddy, flying again after so many days of poor weather. I'm not happy with the weather report, but the airfield meteorologist and I have agreed it would probably improve during the flight.

Mentally thanking my father for his good example, I take my time conducting a routine walk-around inspection. Starting at the propeller, I make sure it is solidly in place. Then to the right wing, checking the flap connections and tracks, moving the aileron up and down. Nothing is binding. No leaks of hydraulic or brake fluids on the landing gear. I walk aft to the rudders and elevators to look for any binding in free-moving control surfaces, then trim tabs for parts or connections that were not secure. I check for water in the gas, and then climb onto the wing and enter the cockpit through the side door.

With a contented sigh, I settle into my seat and breathe deeply. The Spit is a complex aircraft. Its pre-flight cockpit checklist is sixteen steps long. And the engine start-up is another seventeen steps! I've done this often enough to be quick, but never hurried.

Now the engine is primed and flames shoot out the exhaust as the Rolls Royce Merlin engine rumbles to life—with a few momentary flames as the engine warms up. I idle it at 1100 RPM and wait for the oil/coolant temps and pressure to reach proper levels. After a short wait, the oil and coolant gauges reach taxi-ready numbers. I release the brakes and goose the throttle up to 1500 RPM to get her moving, then throttle back down to maintain control. The Spitfire IX is a tricky aircraft to taxi because of the narrow landing gear, the high power of its engine and poor cockpit visibility. I use throttle adjustments along slight left and right turns, to check for obstacles on my way to the runway.

Now that I've reached the runway, I close the canopy, bring the RPM control lever forward, check that the flaps are up, set the elevator and rudder trims, set the super-charger, release the brakes and slowly increase power. As the Spitfire gains speed, the tailwheel leaves the ground. 70…80…90 miles per hour and the Spit breaks free, rising from the ground to do what I want her to do—fly!

She quickly gains speed and altitude. At 140 miles per hour, I gleefully retract the landing gear. As we continue gaining altitude, I adjust the aircraft in the direction of the Aerodrome, enjoying the legendary aircraft's speed and power. I tell her, "Hey girl, I'm sorry I won't get to know you better, but I'm taking you to some boys at the fighter squadron who are very eager to meet you." The need for new equipment, including fighter aircraft like this Spitfire, is dire at this stage of the war.

My instructors' voices drift through my head: "Aviate, navigate, communicate." It strikes me that I'm doing it all on this flight, and still have time to think about what I want to say in a long overdue letter to my mother.

Dearest Mother, if only you knew how happy I am when I fly. I have never felt so completely close to God as when I'm up in the blue. So if you ever get a message that I've

been in a crackup and have been killed, don't grieve for
me more than you can possibly help; just know I died the
way I wanted to.

Flying is, for me, an incurable disease. I need to stay positive now to reassure my family that I'm doing exactly what I love doing. The words to one of my favorite hymns—"When We All Get to Heaven"—pop into my mind, and I sing out loud and off-key to the Heavens above.

About halfway to my destination, the weather becomes frightful and starts to close in around me. A strange mist makes me feel displaced in time and space, as if I'm flying through some primordial world. I shake my head and try to relax.

And then, the plane cuts out on me. It simply refuses to run any longer! I try re-starting the engine…but nothing. I try again.

My magical bird begins to plummet. My school training for surviving crashes races through my head as I struggle to keep calm. Realizing I don't have enough altitude to jump, I know I have to stay with the plane.

Skimming over almost obscured ground too fast to map-read, I keep my eyes on the murky white ground. I am so sure that I'm flying in the right direction that I continue on my path forward.

I don't have time to be frightened. Reminding myself that I love a challenge, I nervously jam two sticks of Wrigley's Double Mint chewing gum into my mouth. I need to concentrate on my landing strategy.

"Dear God, you are my co-pilot," I whisper, now close to tears. "Please keep my mind clear." I'm still guiding my stricken aircraft, gliding through the murk, waiting to break cloud cover. I promise myself to land without tearing up the plane. I have to maintain a safe airspeed and glide path while I find a good landing spot.

How I wish I could speak to someone! But to avoid the Germans, all of us fly without radio contact.

When I fly into a fog bank, I can't see above, below or ahead. "God, I give this to you," I pray out loud, willing myself to stay calm. For a fleeting moment, I feel something soft caressing my cheek.

I look down and realize the fog bank doesn't reach ground level. I feel an odd kinship with the colors of the earth below. They seem intensified, and I can make out a farmer moving slowly back and forth across his hilly field.

Suddenly, a large thatched roof fills the cockpit glass. I try turning to avoid it, but it is already too close! I lower my head and double over, grabbing my seat. At that moment, I hear and feel an enormous BOOM! And then, everything goes black.

TWELVE

Fred Palmer was working in his field when he glanced up and saw the Spitfire coming down from the East, then veer off toward the village of Collingbourne Kingston. He could tell it was in trouble, but was stunned when it crashed into the thatched roof of number 57 on High Street. The impact tore off the roof.

After scattering the roof remains and the upstairs furniture into the road, the aircraft came to rest in the garden of the house next door. The air filled with dust, making it hard to breathe.

Two broad-shouldered Britons rushed to dig out a dead man from the wrecked Spitfire. Instead of a corpse, they found a tiny, self-possessed girl with a mouthful of chewing gum. She had begun crawling toward them when they tried to lift her from the wreckage. She detached her chute unaided, then mumbled a repeated order she had learned from her ATA training: "London, guard that plane."

The young female pilot was carried into what was left of the house and cleaned up on the dining room table while they waited for the ambulance. She was bleeding from the scalp and facial cuts and complained of pain in her thighs where the joy stick had gouged them. She drifted off for about twenty minutes and appeared to have suffered a slight concussion.

Afterward, she explained to the reporters: ""I had hoped to get to the village without tearing up the plane. Instead, I took the second story from a house and sheared off both wings. I rode through the house and wound up in somebody's front yard, right in the middle of their garden. The house I hit came crashing down around their ears and their tea cups," she grinned. "Then I hit a wall and finished off the plane. Only me and the cockpit were left whole."

She continued, "The people living in the house were thrilled to have a plane take off the top of their house, and were even more excited when they saw it was a girl flying the machine—and an American at that! The family had wanted the house rebuilt for years, and now they will get it done for free."

Later she said she didn't remember anything after seeing the roof of the house directly below her, until shortly after she woke up in the hospital. "I knew that I went through the house, lost my wings and finally realized that the aeroplane was a complete write-off. They tell me I spoke to the men who rescued me, ordering them to guard my plane."

The *Macon Telegraph Newspaper* reported:

ATA Second Officer Hazel Raines was transported to Tidworth Military Hospital and received thirteen stitches in her forehead. They shaved off her hair on the right side of her head, thinking she may have been more severely injured than originally appeared. Her knees and legs remained sore and stiff during the two weeks she recovered in hospital.

It's funny, but I don't remember a whole lot about what happened," Hazel admitted, pushing back her little leather skull cap to show them the scars. "This was my first and only crack-up in five years of flying."

She appeared to be suffering vision problems. "The blow seems to have affected my right eye. My vision comes and goes. I must go see an eye specialist in London," she lamented. "All I want to do is go back to work."

Hazel left the hospital ten days later, but remained off duty, due to problems with her right eye. She was not allowed to fly for three months.

THIRTEEN

Mademoiselle Magazine
"The Magazine for Smart Young Women"
February 1943

DIXIE CALLS THE ROLL

It's out of hoop skirts and into dungarees and denims for Southern belles. War has come to Dixieland, and these girls of the Deep South are in it.

There was a time when their background below the Mason Dixon line was a romantic combination of ruffles and moonlight, magnolias and nostalgic melodies of the Land o' Cotton.

But today the Southern belle stands against a wartime background of airplanes, riveting machines, test tubes and codes. She rises before sunup…she's greasy and tired before sundown. She's tight-lipped, determined, but she's enthusiastic. She's at work…at work on a war job.

For women to do their part in wartime is as traditional to the South as corn bread and turnip greens. Our great grandmamas before us, during the War Between the States, melted their prize pewter so their fighting men could have more bullets. That is just one example of how Southern women will stand behind their men at war.

But you are wondering where all these southern girls are working—in what war plants—for the land of Dixie has never boasted of as many factories as farms. The answer is: a boom has swept southward! Furthermore, it's a woman's world in Dixie now. The women are wearing the pants—and literally.

Georgia, you know, is proud of its "firsts" and "onlys," so this state boasts of the fact that Hazel Raines, 26, of Macon, Georgia, is the only girl from the entire southeast working in the British Air Transport Auxiliary. Hazel graduated from the Wesleyan Conservatory (oldest women's college in the U.S.) in '36 and was the first woman in Georgia to secure her commercial pilot's license. She was one of the few women in the country chosen to be an instructor in the Civilian Pilot Training Program, and she held that post until a call came from Jacqueline Cochran, asking if she would join other American women aviators as a flight instructor in the Royal Air Force.

So Hazel took her place in the first line of defense. Her duties as a member of the Air Transport Auxiliary in England are exciting and varied. She moves costly and valuable aircraft; ferries wounded planes fresh from bombings in Germany to a factory for repairs; flies without the aid of radio beams; pilots all types of planes, flying them from factories and stations anywhere in the British Isles…

This magazine article was printed before my accident, so several of my friends and family members sent me copies during my recuperation in the hospital. I couldn't decide if I was pleased with it, annoyed with the writer's sarcasm and perhaps disrespect for southern women, or just upset. I finally determined not to let it bother me, but to just be happy that southern women were getting some of the recognition we deserved.

After being discharged, I returned to Maidenhead and the Littlehales' cozy home and attended a two-week training conversion course. I wouldn't be allowed to fly for three months, but I could take classes as long as I rested in the afternoons.

While living with the Littlehales, a pilot friend gave me a little black Persian kitten. He was so adorable, just nine weeks old and born on the same day as my accident! Naturally I named him "Spitfire." It was quite a sight to see me on the train with Spitfire—sitting up big as you please in a fish basket. I had to change trains twice and in the process, lost my suitcase. Unfortunately, my passport was in it. The bag had no name tag, only a sticker with Southampton on it. I almost went mad when I discovered my loss!

The next morning, the phone rang at 8 a.m. It was the Parcels Room clerk at the station telling me he had found my bag. Thank God! I thanked the clerk, the Lord, and even my mother, who had dashed up to Atlanta one time to pick up a suitcase I left behind there. I've just turned twenty-seven, and am wondering if early memory loss might be the reason for my forgetfulness.

Next week I have several days of leave so my landlady Mrs. Porter and I will visit Oxford. I've often flown over the Spires of Oxford and viewed this "educational center of the world" from the air, and now will be able to enjoy the ordinary layman's perspective.

Three of us received a letter from Jackie Cochran, sent from Fort Worth, Texas on May 20, 1943.

Dear Grace, Hazel and Kay:

I received your thoughtful letters and thank you very much for them. I have hoped for such a long time that I could get back to England, but now that's literally impossible.

The day I arrived home from Britain, I took over the job of the women's flying training program for the Army Air Corps, knowing it would take approximately six months to graduate the first group. At first the Army wanted them to fly only very light equipment, but after much persuasion, I was able to include two-motored training aircraft.

The first group of girls has just graduated and we are waiting for word as to whether they will ferry primary trainers or advanced trainers. We will be turning out several hundred graduates this year—more than six times the number flying for ATA, and I know that with all these available women, we'll get somewhere soon! I am convinced that if you ladies had not gone to England and were not doing the grand job that you do, this program would have never started. It is my strong opinion that you have contributed so much to women in aviation.

I am stationed in Fort Worth, Texas, the headquarters of the Flying Training Command (the largest command in the Army Air Corps) and I find the

Army very cooperative and pleasant to work with. However, I can assure you that it isn't very nice living out in the middle of the country and far from the real activity of the war. How often I wish I were back in England.

Hazel, I heard about your accident and I do hope you have recovered well. Will each of you let me know if there is anything at all I can do for you?

Again, many thanks for your kind thoughts and good wishes,

Jackie

One of the girls in our pool has a home in Cardiff, Wales and invited me to spend three days with her. We went to the horse races in Salisbury and did a little betting. I ended up winning three pounds and twelve shillings! Then we took the train to Langport in Somerset, where we stayed in an old building that Oliver Cromwell had slept in during his battles there. From there, we drove to Musbury—birthplace of the duke of Marlborough. Our next stop was to be Bristol, but while traveling through the gorge, we stopped at a spot known as Burrington Combe—the place where Rev. Toplady took shelter in the crevice of a rock during a storm and composed the famous hymn—"Rock of Ages". All in all, it was a wonderful trip.

I will finally return to duty on June 1. The doctor has given me the okay to fly, so my playing days are over. I'm returning to Maidenhead and finally will be able to follow up on the conversion to Twins. They are restricting me to twin equipment for six months because they think it is better for me not to wear a tight helmet on my head right now. All twin equipment is closed cockpit, and I don't have to wear anything on my head as one must when flying fighters. I am very content with this restriction, because I've waited so long to fly Twins.

FOURTEEN

I had so much news to share with my family and decided to write it all in a letter to Mother, knowing she would pass it around.

June 18, 1943
Dearest Mother,

After spending three months on the ground, I took to the air again two weeks ago! My comprehensive medical exam came out well. I'm flying Twins now, after completing my technical ground work, and already have twenty hours under my belt!

This time I'm living in London and staying at the Red Cross Club. The Littlehales' son is on leave from the Navy and staying with them, so there's no room at the inn. I ride the train to work and back, and my commute is about an hour each way. The food is very good at the club and we can even buy Coca-Colas there! Such a treat!

Mother, you know my contract expires October 14. Well, after much thought and prayer, I've signed up for six additional months. This will extend my contract until next April. I applied for a month's leave to return to the U.S. to visit you and the family, and they gave me the month of September. I hope to see y'all the second week in September.

I'm so sad to tell you that my kitty Spitfire got the cat flu last week and died. Poor little thing; we did everything we could to save him but he was so small and wasn't strong enough to survive. I will miss him very much, but still have my dog Scottie, and recently bought two liver and white cocker spaniels. They came in a pair, are three months old and are adorable! Mrs. Porter is swell to let me have so many animals around and take care of them when I'm away. I really love having pets.

You do remember that I bought a bicycle? Well, a couple of girls from the pool and I cycled seventy-five miles in two and a half days. It was such a wonderful ride, but now I'm very sore. We spent two nights down by the seaside and it was so peaceful I almost felt like I was home again.

Speaking of home, I went by the Embassy and had my passport put in proper order for the return trip to Georgia. Gee, I can hardly wait! It won't be long now, I'm sure. I should see you by September 18—so keep your fingers crossed!

I was back in Georgia much sooner than I expected. My doctor examined me after my complaints of blurred vision in my right eye and poor depth perception. We agreed that I should immediately return to Georgia and take care of it there.

I flew to New York on August 6th and was in Macon the next evening. I was so surprised to wake up actually enjoying the sweltering Macon summer sun. This was the first time I'd been hot since leaving a year and a half earlier. I told my family that everyone is still wearing wool sweaters and often an overcoat in England even now. We had a good laugh over that.

My eleven-year-old niece Fabi asked me this morning if the Brits liked having Americans fighting with them.

"Oh yes. They're quite happy to have us there. They really like us but can't get used to the Yanks' boisterous high spirits."

"What food have you been dying to eat here?" My sister Frankie wanted to know.

"I'd love to have Cokes and hot dogs," I grinned. "Then a platter of Mother's fried chicken, which I've missed like crazy."

"And what will you do here for fun?" Martha wondered.

"Mostly laugh, eat, and hang out with y'all. Oh, and enjoy American shampoo and getting a permanent wave."

Mother seemed a little anxious. "And you promise to rest as well, right?"

I nodded. "Yes, Mother. A rest is what I'm home for, and I'm really looking forward to it. But that can include games, cards, books, and everything I can do with my family."

I added, more seriously, "You have no idea how much I missed you—your voices, laughter and hugs."

Looking around the living room, I felt deeply grateful to be here again, surrounded by my family. I'd been through so much in the past four months, yet was always sustained by their cheerful letters, gifts, and now...their encouragement.

The month flew by. I traveled to Miami and around Florida, giving speeches, seeing old pilot friends I taught with, and attending the wedding of a former flying pupil in

Miami. I was also a guest speaker at a dinner meeting of the *Ninety-Niners* in Jacksonville. Mother has promised to join me on my next trip to Miami. We've decided to spend a week fishing, swimming and sunning.

I was always happy to get news from England and Texas. About a year ago, Jackie Cochran had been named Director of the *Women's Airforce Service Pilots, or WASP,* and now is about to move her training base from Howard Hughes Field in Houston to Avenger Field in Sweetwater, Texas. She telephoned me with the exciting news.

"Hello, Hazel. I'm delighted to hear you are doing well and enjoying your visit stateside," she said. "You've resolved that problem with your eyes, right? I'm hoping you'll want to stay a while longer." I could feel the smile in her voice.

"Hi, Jackie! Yes, my eyes are back to normal. The month-long family reunion has been perfect, but I do miss you and flying."

"Of course you do. I've been contacting your friends at the ATA and now would like to offer you work here in Texas. I need girls who have a lot of flying experience to show the country just how well women fly. Two of your friends have already accepted, and I'm hoping you will join us as well."

Inhaling deeply, I was at a loss of words. Finally, I answered. "Oh, Jackie, would we doing the same type of flying as we did there? Will I fly Twins and…"

"Hazel, I've organized a new training program that follows exactly the Air Force Cadet Program of primary, basic, and advanced flight training and ground school. Even the training aircraft are the same."

She laughed knowingly. "There will be much to learn, but yes, you'll be flying. Think about it and get back to me when you have decided. And either way, Hazel Jane, I will fully support your decision."

FIFTEEN

Jackie Cochran was a very interesting woman. Born an orphan, (she told us she never knew who her parents were) she grew up in foster homes in the lumber mill towns of Florida. She learned to fight for what she wanted at a very young age. Later she studied hairdressing and cosmetics and worked in beauty salons until starting her own Cochran Cosmetic Company.

When Jackie decided to fly, she quickly broke records for altitude. She entered and won transcontinental speed races, formerly open only to men. Her husband, businessman Floyd Odlum, encouraged her ambitions and stood behind her all the way.

During an informal social event, she told us she learned to fly during a Christmas holiday, paying for her own lessons. In three weeks, she had her pilot's license. "A beauty operator ceased to exist, and an aviator was born."

After Jackie and Floyd married in 1936, she hired a private detective to trace her natural parents. When she handed Floyd the report, it was unread and in a sealed envelope. Neither of them ever opened it. Floyd's money, contacts and business expertise enabled Jackie to use their wealth to live her independent lifestyle and pursue her groundbreaking ambitions.

Like her friend Amelia Earhart, she believed in extrasensory perception. Jackie and her husband claimed they could communicate mentally when they were apart or even during sleep.

Amelia and her husband George Putman spent several days in 1937 relaxing at the Coachella Ranch—Jackie and Floyd's home in Southern California. Amelia knew she must be alert and rested before her big flight. Based on a premonition from the night before, Jackie tried to convince Amelia to postpone flying the next day. Jackie's hunches were usually accurate, but everyone hoped she would be proven wrong this time.

After his wife went missing, George Putnam prayed that Jackie's psychic powers could help him find Amelia's aircraft. For several days, Jackie tried to visualize where Amelia and her co-pilot were located. Yet in the end, she told him she had lost all connection. She said she "saw" Earhart after her plane went down, and somehow learned that Amelia's last words were "Circling—circling, cannot see island—gas running low."

Those were the last words anyone heard from Amelia. "That still hurts," Jackie told us. Finally accepting that her dear friend was no longer alive, Jackie lit a candle for her. So shaken by the experience, she vowed never to use her psychic powers again.

With her husband's encouragement, she raced airplanes and broke records. In 1938, she became the second woman to win the Bendix Race. The judge who drove out to congratulate her on the runway had to wait while she repaired her makeup. She went on to develop a very successful brand of beauty products that moisturized dry skin and soothed chapped lips. Because she loved to share, she gifted these products to her students.

At the beginning of the Second World War, civilian pilots were grounded. Fortunately, Jackie had a successful cosmetics business. But she was determined to find a way into the war as a pilot. She did everything possible to make that happen, starting at the top with General Arnold in America and Lord Beaverbrook in England.

They finally agreed to let her fly a bomber across the Atlantic. Several military pilots were so incensed that a civilian pilot—and a woman at that—would undertake such a flight, that she agreed to let a male pilot handle the take-off and landing. Soon after arriving in England, she met with Pauline Gower, leader of the female ferry pilots at the Air Transport Auxiliary.

Back in the United States, she was invited to the White House to discuss the possible role of female pilots in the war. The decision was made that it was not yet time to use American female pilots at home. Two weeks later, Jackie escorted a group of women to Britain to join the *British Air Transport Auxiliary* (**ATA**), and I was one of the chosen twenty-five pilots in that first group.

In the fall of 1942, Jackie again returned to the U.S., where she learned that Nancy Love, a rival whom she recognized as "an exceedingly fine pilot," was already setting up a *Women's Auxiliary Ferrying Squadron* (**WAFS**) for the Army. Jackie felt that position should have been hers, and went directly to General Hap Arnold for an explanation.

It was eventually sorted out. Nancy continued with her operation while Jackie set up a training school for women who had fewer than 500 hours of flying time. Her group was called the *Women's Flying Training Detachment* (**WFTD**) and headquartered in Houston, Texas. She later moved it to Sweetwater, Texas: a smaller airport that was better suited for training.

Jackie Cochran insisted on strict military discipline, even though these women were civilians. These two groups soon combined to form the *Women's Airforce Service Pilots* (**WASP**). They worked as ferry pilots and instructors, and also towed targets for student anti-aircraft gunners, engineered test flights, replicated gas attacks, performed day and night training missions for radar, and simulated low-level strafing (legalized buzzing). These women flew every kind of Army Air Corps plane that existed.

Jacqueline kept in touch with her students in the U.S. and England. She had plans for them.

So the day she phoned and asked me if I'd like to remain in the U.S. and work for her, of course I said "YES!"

SIXTEEN

Jacqueline Cochran got what she asked for. Her training center was moved four hundred miles northwest from Houston to Avenger Field in Sweetwater, Texas. Applicants to this training school needed a pilot's license, but the flight time requirement was reduced from seventy-five to thirty-five hours. (Men entering the same training schools needed no pilot's license and no flight time at all.) The first group to arrive at Avenger Field found a class of male cadets training to be transport pilots. The men remained at the field for about two weeks after the women arrived, so this would be the first co-educational flight training in the history of the American armed forces.

In February of 1943, Avenger Field became an all-female installation, except for a few male instructors and officers who lived off base. The field was officially assigned to the 318th Army Air Corps Flying Training Detachment. The WASPs remained civilians, but Jackie was working diligently to militarize them like other women's auxiliaries. We students were working too hard to even think about that.

Jackie refused to compromise in her physical requirements. She arranged for a physical exam (identical to those given to the Army Air Corps cadets) to be offered at air bases near the trainees' homes. This was called the "Form 64"—designed for prospective combat pilots. She wanted her women to be equal to their male counterparts.

The day we arrived, we quickly discovered that Sweetwater was known for its rattlesnakes, tarantulas, black widows and scorpions. We experienced first-hand the constant dusty wind and very warm temperatures—close to one hundred degrees most of the year.

"You'll get used to getting Texas dust in your teeth," one of the students told us as we unpacked in the barracks. "But check for scorpions in your boots every morning before you put them on." She had been one of the first trainees to arrive and was happy to see us.

Ugh! What a welcome! Another girl told me that locusts could work their way under the sheets, get into your hair and were so thick on the runway that planes could skid on them during landings. What had we gotten ourselves into?

Each barrack had a housemother, like at college dormitories. We quickly learned the rules. We weren't allowed to smoke in town and were told to dress modestly and nicely when we went off base. "Don't socialize too much," warned our housemother. When we rolled our eyes at that, she added, "These are not my rules. They come from Miss Jacqueline Cochran." Soon we were calling Avenger Field "Cochran's Convent."

We knew our program would be demanding, but some of us had already been through similar regimens in England. A few women quit and several washed out, which was everyone's nightmare. Yet the graduation rate for trainees was seventy-four percent for the 1943 graduates, and during my graduating year, 1944, it was eighty-three percent. This is considerably higher than for male trainees in the Central Flying Training Command in 1944.

What we resented the most was abusive behavior by some male instructors. One of our best students, who was "washed out," suspected it had happened because she wouldn't let an instructor kiss her. Jackie immediately launched an investigation.

A review board confirmed that this instructor and a few others had targeted pilots who refused to date them. The board instituted changes so trainees who failed with one instructor could train with another and be re-assessed. This slowed down the "unearned failures" imposed by unprofessional instructors.

None of us from ATA faced those problems, because everyone had seen how well we handled our planes. In fact, our instructors were delighted that we flew so expertly.

"You know, I sort of feel sorry for these instructors," my classmate Dorothy told me. "Imagine being supermen and all of a sudden, some girls arrive and are doing the same thing; sometimes, even better."

We worked very hard, both physically and mentally. Our physical training class was rigid, and we followed the same procedures as the male pilots. But in our free time, we started a WASP newspaper with articles about movie reviews, book reviews, flying and war news. On nice days off, we even sunbathed: discreetly, of course.

We made up new lyrics for tunes of already popular songs. "The Battle Hymn of the Republic" became "*We Were Only Foolin'*" and began with "When we go to ground school we're as happy as can be…"

And this was our version of "*Yankee Doodle Dandy.*"

We are Yankee Doodle Pilots
Yankee Doodle do or die.
Real live nieces of our Uncle Sam
Born with a yearning to fly.
Keep in step to all our classes
March to Flight Line with our pals,
Yankee Doodle came to Texas
Just to fly the "PTs"
We are those Yankee Doodle Gals!

And we had *Fifinella.* Many army units adopted mascots—cartoon figures that informally identified the unit. We weren't military, but we did come up with a mascot.

Fifinella was a female gremlin created by Roald Dahl in his first children's book, *The Gremlins.* He had joined the Royal Air Force in 1939 when the war began. He listened to the tales British airmen told about impish creatures who played tricks and sabotaged their planes. He was seriously injured after his plane crashed in the Sahara. During his recovery, he wrote about gremlins and female gremlins—*Fifinellas.*

After his stories were published, Walt Disney suggested making an animated film based on the story. The film was never made, but Disney released these stories as a book with illustrations by a Walt Disney animator.

The WASPs asked Disney for permission to use *Fifi* as their mascot, and he happily agreed. We thought of *Fifi* as nice, but impish. She was a shapely female gremlin wearing a short red dress and red boots, gold tights, a gold helmet and blue goggles. She was our protector, and welcomed everyone who entered Avenger Field with a smile on her goggled face. Class after class smiled back at her.

November 4, 1943

Dearest Mother,

At last: a spare moment to tell you I'm O.K. They keep us so busy here at Avenger Field. We get up at 6 a.m., breakfast at 6:35, on the Flight Line at 7:30 to 1 p.m., eat at 1:15, Ground School at 1:55, Physical Training at 5:15, Supper at 6:40, and back to quarters by 8. We have two hours before lights out at 10 o'clock, but we all study then.

Some of our subjects are Math, Physics, Navigation, Meteorology, Aircraft Engines, etc. and on weekends we must attend lectures on Military Subjects. It is a rigid schedule, and we have to march in flight formations to everything. I know it is good training and I hope I can continue to take it. Quite different from England in so many ways.

The food is wonderful, and I don't think I'll need my ration book here. There are five other girls in my room and they all seem to be very nice.

My new job is Post Bugler. I like it even though I have to get up at 5:45. We'll be flying in a couple of days, so that gives us all something to look forward to.

There was no standard uniform when the first class arrived. Any combination of civilian clothing (except cowboy boots) was allowed. Soon cotton mechanic's overalls, and later white turbans, were required wear during duty hours. Jackie demanded a professional military appearance for her ladies, and we soon bought khaki cotton trousers with a while shirt and a khaki overseas cap.

In the spring of 1944, every woman will be issued dress and flight uniforms and flight coveralls of Santiago blue, similar to French ultramarine blue. The dress uniform will consist of a straight, knee-length skirt and a belted jacket worn with an oxford-cloth blue or white shirt and black tie. The flight uniform will be slacks and a short Eisenhower jacket, with the blue shirt either open at the neck or with the tie.

And Mother, we've seen the photos of this ensemble. We shall look very elegant in our dress uniform! We will wear a beret, pulled to the right, with a gold U.S. coat of arms pinned front and center. Our insignia includes gold lapel wings and prints spelling out "WASP." A black over-the-shoulder purse, black shoes, and gray overcoat will complete the outfit.

Jackie was here to greet us when we arrived, and we love being with her again. Apparently she's not on site that much, but we are enjoying her now.

We have a rigid inspection on Saturdays and everything must be spotless. If they find any dirt anywhere, or your bed is made wrong, you get demerits and are confined to Post for the weekend. Last week, our bay (room) was the only one that didn't get a single demerit. I imagine you can't believe that, but know that we are all walking the straight and narrow so we can go into town next weekend. They make everyone wait for two weeks, but we're almost there!

Sending all my love to you and family,

Hazel Jane

SEVENTEEN

In the early spring of 1944, bad weather grounded four WASPs in Americus, Georgia. They left their airplanes in the hanger at the airport and caught a bus into town to find a hotel room. While walking down the main street, they were stopped by a police car. One officer got out of the car and demanded they accompany him to the police station.

"What have we done?" The bravest one asked.

"Ma'am, women are not allowed in the street wearing slacks at night," he said sternly.

No amount of insisting that they were Army pilots in uniform would convince them.

The women were locked in a cell. They asked to make a telephone call to the ferrying base. Instead, the officer tested their story by calling the Commanding Officer of the air base where they had landed. Unfortunately, the Commanding Officer was at a party.

The WASPs listened to the sheriff's end of the conversation with growing alarm.

"We have a few girls down here impersonating officers," he said.

Because he enunciated the last two words in a mocking tone, the WASPs realized the sheriff thought they were "women of the street."

"Yes, Sir. That's exactly where I've got them: locked up."

After 2:00 in the morning they were they were allowed to make one phone call. They decided to wake up Nancy Love in Cincinnati, since they knew Jackie Cochran was in England.

Nancy Love was furious and demanded to speak to the sheriff. The WASPs were finally released and driven back to the airfield, where they sat uncomfortably until dawn, when they were allowed to take off. They wanted to fly as far away from Americus as possible.

We hated to hear stories like this. Fortunately, they were rare. But sometimes the WASPs were denied accommodations at the huge USAAF bases where they put down to *Remain over Night* (RON). Then we had to find accommodations at our own expense.

We learned to iron our shirts and collars on hotel radiators, to press slacks under mattresses, and other resourceful tricks. Eventually, we learned to sleep in airport lobbies.

At the better bases, especially where we flew frequently, accommodations might be in the Bachelor Officers' Quarters. Military operations could become humorous also. A flight of WASPs flying Cubs was forced down at the Marine base in Quantico, Virginia, because of weather. The Marines were anxious to be hospitable. They partitioned off part of the barracks with a sturdy wall and posted a sign: KEEP OUT! LADIES PRESENT. The officer on duty even posted an armed guard, who personally escorted each of the ladies to the latrine.

It's been cold here in Sweetwater this November. My "long-handles" sure help keep me warm. I have been flying early, first period, between 7:45 and 9:00 a.m. It's a great time of the day to be up. Today there was almost a solid overcast at about 1,500 feet, so we climbed up to 8,000 feet where the clouds below looked like a fluffy white blankets. Then the sun came up and burned holes in the blanket, causing the clouds to slowly roll up in odd individual shapes and gracefully float away.

I'm missing my family, but my barrack-mates have become new friends. We often go away on Saturday or Sunday to the "big city of Sweetwater." Five of us went last Saturday and enjoyed our typical afternoon shopping tour. It was great fun to sit in the corner drug store, drinking Cokes and sharing stories.

"Hazel, I'll bet you were a leader in high school and college, weren't you?" Meg asked.

I laughed. "You would be surprised. I was more scholarly in high school, but I came out a little more in college. Why do you ask?"

"Well, we look to you for advice and support when we need it," offered Linda, a quiet young lady from Nebraska.

I grinned. "Let me tell you how it was for me. I was always courteous to teachers and classmates, but I rushed home from school every day to do my homework, read and help Mother get dinner on the table. I didn't like to gossip, so I didn't walk home with the girls who did. But during my senior year, I discovered that most of my classmates liked me."

"What do you mean?"

"One of them scrawled a funny comment under my yearbook photo: '*Flash Raines, the most likely person to get anywhere first!*' And others added nice comments and warm wishes for my future."

They laughed and we shared other stories of our high school and college days. It felt so good to be with fellow pilots—my new friends. We had similar goals! I felt happy. I was definitely where I wanted to be.

Ground school is harder than I had expected. I'm working really hard to pass Math and Physics. They posted grades for the first two weeks and mine were not so good: Math 70, Physics 85 and Theory of Flight 90. I have to bear down and bring up the first two.

Mrs. Deaton, Director of the school here, has asked me to talk on Tuesday night to the American Legion Post in Sweetwater, and I said yes. I thought my speech-making days would be over once I got here, but I'm really okay with it. I'm also going to give a short talk here at our Thanksgiving service in the gym. I wonder if they've asked me because I have been flying longer than most trainees.

Today we started new classes in Code, Navigation and Aircraft Engines. Now this is more up my alley! Anything to do directly with aircraft interests me, whereas Math and Physics simply do not. This is just the type of training I've always wanted to take. If I'd gone to a private school, like Spartan Aviation School in Oklahoma, this course would have cost $35,000! And, I will get my instrument rating if I stay here and take the full course. That's worth everything to me!

We've just about finished our primary training, 70 hours in a Stearman—a biplane with an open cockpit—as cold as can be. We're given two civilian and one Army fight check during those 70 hours. I did fine on my first and second civilian checks and have the Army ride next week. I think I'll be finished by early January.

I'm going to ask my mother to make me a pound cake and send it here to share with the girls. She really makes the best one I've ever tasted. And I know that I won't be able to go home for Christmas, so that treat should make us all feel closer to our families. I'm happy remembering the wonderful moments we shared over the summer, and know I'll see my family again sometime in 1945.

The weather continues to plague us. We had rain and snow last week, and things were very mucky. But they're planning a big party over the Christmas celebration, and we'll have about one-hundred-and-fifty flying officers and cadets here for a huge Christmas dinner/dance. They're coming from a nearby Aerodrome, so we'll have more than enough dancing partners.

They're also putting up Christmas decorations and a tree or two, so I expect they are doing their best to make it a joyous Christmas away from our families. I have found a nice Methodist Church here that reminds me of my church in Macon: Vineville United Methodist. So, I'll be able to celebrate the real reason for Christmas—if not with my family, at least with friends.

EIGHTEEN

I t's January 10th, 1944: my seventh year in Aviation. I'm proud and relieved to have survived 70 hours in an open plane in cold weather. Who knew Texas could be so cold? Last night's snow storm left everything hidden under a white blanket. Soon it will melt and leave the ground a wet, soupy, slushy mess.

Finishing up my last test flight was difficult since I was cold for so long. My mind kept telling me I couldn't do it—but I told myself, Yes you can! And I did! My instructors were all pleased with me and with all of *Class 44-W-4*. Every one of us passed with flying colors!

I've been elected President of the Welfare Board. That means I take care of the general welfare of the "student body" here, and organize the entertainment for Avenger Field. I will also speak at civic meetings when invited. I enjoy that, since I've realized I can tell my stories well and without stage fright. Daddy was a member of the Macon Lions Club. He also spoke to groups and once took me to a dinner meeting, which was really fun. Maybe I inherited this from him?

How I wish he were with me. When I wonder why I have been given so many breaks, I remember my father's words: *Do everything in an honest and sincere manner. Give it all you've got.* Because I truly love flying, I do put everything I've got into it. I know Daddy is proud of me, and I imagine he's smiling from the Heavens while his spirit joins me on all my flights.

Unexpectedly, I'm feeling overcome by a special memory of home.

My family was so excited at the news of my becoming the first female pilot in Georgia to be licensed. The Sunday after my ceremony, we celebrated it with a special dinner of one of our favorite meals: Mother's smothered chicken with rice and okra.

As we were clearing the table, Daddy heard a gentle knock on the door and went to see who it was. He was surprised to see Ann Daniels, who lived in a house he had remodeled years earlier. She went to the kitchen to give a quick peck to Mother, then held me at arms' length with a big smile.

"Congratulations, Hazel Jane. I am so sorry to barge in, Mrs. Raines, but George and I speak frequently of Frank, and this seemed like a good time to renew our friendship. So I've brought you some Toll House cookies as a contribution to the festivities."

She held my hand in hers. "Dear Hazel Jane, your father was such a pleasure to work with," she said, as my mother pulled back the napkin covering the basket filled with cookies, then placed a fresh cup of tea on the lace tablecloth.

"What might have been a stressful construction experience turned into an unforgettable party. Frank would always show up with a big smile, funny stories and sometimes a song or two. Every time we look out our window, we feel like he's still out there, admiring his handiwork over our shoulders."

Daddy looked up at her and smiled. "No man could dream of feeling more happiness on this day," he said quietly.

"My wife and daughters have gotten by without things they wanted and deserved for many years, because my business wasn't always successful."

After a thoughtful pause, I spoke.

"Daddy, we were brought together by God this afternoon to give warm thanks for our many blessings. Your kind heart, desire to see a smile on every face and pride in doing the best job possible have always inspired us to live up to your shining example. Every time I fly, you will be sitting there too and, with God's grace, will continue guiding me as you always have. Not a man alive has achieved more success than you."

I believe I'll always carry those words in my heart.

March 10, 1944

Dearest Mother:

I have been working very hard on the instrument flying course. When I finish, I will be able to handle aeroplanes under almost any weather condition, good or bad. By the time you receive this letter, I hope my good break has come through.

There is a graduation class tomorrow (the third) and Jackie is here for the event. She invited me for lunch (in town) and suggested an alternative to my graduating in May. It would cut my training short by two months; so once I've completed my instrument training course, I could graduate with the next class: 44-W-3, rather than my original class.   She could exempt me from the cross- country flying, since I did so much of that in England.

"Then I could send you to B-26 Marauder (heavy twin-engine bomber) transition school for nine weeks," Jackie announced.

I was speechless. I didn't know what to say. She noticed.

"You have time to think about this, Hazel." She grinned. "Until tomorrow. Oh, and if you choose to go, you'll have your choice of serving here in the U.S. or foreign duty. I hear Australia is nice."

I loved her sense of humor. "You've convinced me, Jackie. I'll work hard and graduate early. Thank you very much for giving me this chance."

"Hazel, you have earned it. I'm happy for you and very proud of you."

So I finished the instrument course and my 35 hours of final check rides. You won't believe this, Mother, but it's true. **I made the highest grade ever given here at the field in flying of any type!** *And I made it on an instrument ride! The check pilot was so pleased and excited over the ride I gave him that he read my flight report to the entire class. I know God was sitting up there with me the whole time! So was Daddy.*

I love you, Hazel

NINETEEN

HEADQUARTERS, ARMY AIR CORPS
April 7, 1944
Dear Miss Raines,

I have your very nice letter of March 28th. I am so glad to know you have derived so much benefit from the course there. Naturally, we are pretty proud of it.

I doubt very much I will be able to attend the graduation in April, what with our bill languishing in the House and much work still to be done. It will be a wonderful thing for all of us to get this bill passed.

There won't be a class of B-26 students going in this month.

I hope your first assignment after graduation will be to your liking and satisfaction. If any girls are assigned to low target squadrons, they will fly only good equipment.

Here's hoping everything will go well with you in the future. Kind personal regards.

Sincerely,
Jacqueline Cochran, Director of Women Pilots

I knew that the letter's serious and formal tone was because she felt others might read it. Jackie was working so hard to get a bill passed in the House that would militarize the WASPs.

Some publications, like *Time Magazine*, were turning public opinion against the WASPs. In a May 29, 1944 *Time Magazine* article titled "Unnecessary and Undesirable", the writer said the WASPs' experiment had been expensive and that men could have been trained more quickly and cheaply.

The instructors, civilian pilots and military men being turned down for military pilot's training had become the WASPs' biggest opponents. They wrote letters to their representatives and raised money for lobbyists to influence other members of Congress. Jackie imposed a "gag order" on us: *keep quiet, avoid interviews with the press, and do not write to your representatives.* Of course we followed her order.

The press was even worse. Instead of reporting on the WASPs' skills, experience, and hard work, most articles focused on the women's figures and faces. Such biased "glamour-girl" pieces gave the public a very superficial and inaccurate view of the women's program. No matter how much some articles praised our skills and dedication, we were always girl pilots, distinctly different from the "real thing."

My graduation was a sad affair (personally) without Jackie, but we enjoyed looking snappy in our new uniforms. And the best thing of all is that *Fifinella* is still with us! Walt Disney designed a special insignia for us: *Fifi*, complete with goggles and her own wings! We wear her patch on our jackets, right next to our wings.

I have just moved to Pecos, Texas and will be working at the Army Air Field here. I am now a test pilot, and the work is interesting, exciting, and fun. I love it! We test fly the aircraft after repairs have been made, and so far, I've tested light twin-engine UC-78s. Our work day begins at 7:30 a.m. and is usually finished by 4 p.m. We have Saturday afternoons and Sundays off: more free time than I got in other bases (except final training). There are only seven of us here, and I am the Squadron Commander.

I missed the girls in my original training class (before Jackie moved me to another one to graduate early), so I flew back to Sweetwater to attend their graduation. I still consider myself part of that group, just an "early release". I was able to spend some time with Jackie, who is quite frustrated about the battle for militarization. If or when we do get military status, I will go to Orlando, Florida for officer training. Then I would be able to spend a few days at home in Georgia!

It's hot and dusty in Pecos. I've decided I prefer English fog to Texan dust. Some days it gets up to 120 degrees around noon. I should be leaving around the first of July, and am now helping with some ferrying flights. A few weeks ago, several of us ferried ships to New Mexico and spent the day in Santa Fe. What a lovely town that is! We stayed on a ranch, rode horses, and fished—I caught five mountain trout. I thought about my parents constantly since they both loved fishing. The trout I caught tasted so much better than the trout we buy in Macon.

We were told we would be getting military status soon, so I've been in Orlando for two weeks already! Everything happened so fast! I'm already halfway through the tactical training all WASPs will now receive. I arrived at 7:30 a.m. one Wednesday morning and was in class two hours later.

I'm taking a ground school course for prospective officers in the Army Air Corps: eight hours of daily classes for four weeks. The course is interesting and calls for hours of hard work and studying, but since I've never done this type of work, I'm enjoying it.

By August 18th, I had completed my training in Orlando, visited my family in Macon and returned to Pecos Army Air Field as the Squadron Commander. That promotion was short-lived. I soon received orders to leave west Texas and report to Kingman Army Air Field in Arizona by September 18, 1944. My pay grade will remain the same as my promotion pay. My job here is to tow targets in B-26s for the gunners in the B-17s to shoot at. The target trails behind us about 500 feet.

Towing targets is often misunderstood. We know it can be dangerous, and understand the risks are greater than most women would be willing to take. Yet most of us gladly accept them, so male pilots can fight the war. Sometimes we feel like clay pigeons at a county fair shooting gallery, or even sitting ducks. We try not to complain. We're in the Army now...

When we finish our course around October 12th, I think we might be going to Lincoln, Nebraska. Although our working days are shorter here (we finish at about five o'clock), we are now flying every day. Yesterday we flew up to Boulder Dam and Las Vegas, Nevada—just to see them from the air. We fly over California every day, sometimes as far as Los Angeles. All of this is so beautiful. The views are spectacular! I try to remember to count my blessings every day.

TWENTY

We joined the WASPs to serve our country. And we have. Women can fly as well as men. At the final graduation of the WASP cadets, General Hap Arnold spoke.

"You, and more than nine-hundred of your sisters, have shown that you can fly wingtip to wingtip with your brothers. If ever there was a doubt in anyone's mind that women can become skillful pilots, the WASPs have dispelled that doubt.

Frankly, I didn't know in 1941 whether a slip of a young girl could fight the controls of a B-17 in the heavy weather they would naturally encounter in operational flying. Those of us who have been flying for twenty or thirty years know that flying an airplane is something you do not learn overnight.

Well, now in 1944, more than two years since WASPs first started flying with the Air Forces, we can come to only one conclusion—the entire operation has been a success. It is on the record that women can fly as well as men.

Certainly we haven't been able to build an airplane you can't handle. From AT-6s to B-29s, you have flown them around like veterans. One of the WASPs has even test-flown our new jet plane. So, on this final graduation day of our program, I salute you and all WASPs. We of the AAF are proud of you; we will never forget our debt to you."

Despite such support from the General, dark clouds were looming on the horizon. Two of our best pilots had quit: Marion Hanrahan and Marie Shale. Mabel Rawlinson and her instructor were killed when their plane shuddered in midair, causing the landing gear to hit the tops of some sea pines. It plummeted straight down and crashed into the swamp at the edge of the field. On impact, the A-24 Dauntless cracked in two and the front half burst into flames, killing them instantly.

After this accident, the deplorable conditions of the airplanes at Camp Davis came to light, Jackie Cochran immediately arrived to launch an investigation. She learned that eleven pilots had suffered forced landings, and the WASPs were spending endless hours flying over the swamps looking for downed planes. Some tires on the planes were so old that we had five blowouts in one day. Few radios worked.

The newly graduated pilots of the final WASP training class were sent to Camp Davis in North Carolina, and after an accelerated preparation course, joined us in the air. We were happy to have them.

One afternoon pilot Kay Menges returned from ferrying and found Camp Davis in an uproar. Everyone looked upset, running around with long faces. There had been another crash—another pilot was killed. Kay had seen an A-24 on its back in the grass as she circled the field to land.

She ran into one of the WASPs, Helen Snapp. Helen kept pacing back and forth near the barracks door, as if willing her friend to walk in. "Betty was my best friend in training and here too," she sobbed. "And she'd just gotten married."

"I'm so sorry, Helen." Kay murmured, gently reaching for her hand.

"I've never felt so distressed and heartbroken about anything in my life," she cried, in a voice we'd never heard before. "Why is everything going wrong now?"

Kay slid her arm around Helen and offered her a tissue. "I don't know," she said softly. "But we're all here with you, and we'll try to find a way to work this out."

Helen's sobbing stopped, but she kept searching the sky through the window, as if looking for an answer that would never come.

Kay waited until Helen had calmed down, then paid a visit to the mechanics to find out what had happened to Betty's airplane. She remembered the day she flew an A-24 with a sticky throttle. After she hit the throttle, the plane did not respond for several seconds. Suddenly, it roared forward and lurched into a climb. She then had to put all her weight onto the right rudder or the violent torque of the propeller would have spun the plane over.

The mechanics told her that on final approach, Betty had announced a go-around. But instead of roaring into a climb, the plane hit the runway hard, bounced and flipped over. It came crashing to the ground on its canopy top.

"May I please see the Form One?" she asked one of them.

What she saw made her sick. It was her own handwriting: "Sticky Throttle." Turning to him, she asked, "Has this been repaired since this report?"

He shook his head. "I'm so sorry. We never received any orders to do it."

Kay could hear the pounding of her heart and tried to slow its beats. She felt a lump in her throat and swallowed hard. *I will not cry. I'm a grown woman, for God's sake.*

She realized Betty would not have known how to correct this delayed surge of power after gunning the engine for her go-around. "Thank you for your help," she told the mechanic, leaving quietly.

Walking past planes parked in a hangar, Kay felt a sense of danger she'd never experienced before.

Jackie returned to Camp Davis the next day. She experienced firsthand the debilitating sorrow triggered by the death of the quiet young California pilot. The girls were learning the hard way that they had to protect themselves, know the peculiarities of a red-lined airplane, and refuse to fly when they didn't trust one.

The unhappiness and sense of despair deeply affected Jackie, who investigated Betty Taylor's death herself. After the funeral the following day, she left Camp Davis, without a word about her findings. What she had uncovered could not be discussed. She asked the mechanics who were present at the briefing to keep quiet and not frighten the girls. Jackie believed if the women learned the true cause of the accident, there might be an insurrection, and the entire WASP program could be endangered.

The mechanics had actually discovered traces of sugar in the demolished A-24's gas tank. It could take as little as one teaspoon to stop an engine in seconds. The "sticky throttle" Kay warned of now had ominous implications. Jackie was convinced it had been sabotage. She didn't know more than that, and chose to move forward at this time.

Every WASP member had volunteered for this hazardous duty to support the War effort. Jackie was stunned and heartbroken to realize that some of those admired male pilots resented the WASPs enough to wish them death or injury. It belied the comforting sense of solidarity against an evil enemy.

A similar fatal accident suffered by another female pilot led to the Camp Davis commanding officer's disastrous order. WASPs would remain at the base, but could only be "co-pilots" or "replacement pilots" on larger twin-engine C-45 transports or B-34 medium-gray bombers.

Since the WASPs jumped up to volunteer every time the operations officer proposed a flying mission, some male pilots realized they could keep playing cards and let the women do the flying. Some days, the WASPs flew a morning and then an afternoon flight, for up to six hours a day in the air. What had been intended as a demotion had become a blessing.

Male pilots were slowly becoming fond of us. When one of them was granted the transfer he'd requested in protest of our presence on base, he turned it down. "Well, Sir," he said, "we think maybe we'd better stick around here and see that these girls get through this damned course."

By now, many male pilots have already returned to the U.S. to resume military and civilian duties. I wonder how deeply that will affect the WASPs' program.

TWENTY-ONE

Public opinion shifted, and the men who wanted our jobs began a concerted attack. They had won over many publications and veterans' organizations. They complained to their Congressional representatives that the WASPs were taking jobs that should be theirs. One member of Congress, Representative Robert Ramspeck, supported us and decided to set up an investigative committee. His plan to support our program backfired.

Not one committee member ever visited Avenger Field. Nor did anyone visit a single base where WASPs were stationed. They never talked to us or to Jackie Cochran. But they produced a detailed report, based solely on the male pilots' complaints.

A few members of the committee disagreed with the report's conclusions and voted not to accept the Ramspeck Report, but the majority voted in support of it. Their conclusion: the WASP program had never been necessary. No mention was made that the War Department, the Army Air Corps, and General Arnold all disagreed with this conclusion. They all insisted it was needed.

The report stated, "There is every reason to believe that the induction of additional unskilled personnel will accelerate the accident and fatality rate." But the Army Air Corps' records had proved that women had a lower accident and fatality rate than men. The truth didn't seem to matter.

The House of Representatives' Committee on Appropriations also issued a report. Their members voted unanimously in favor of this report's conclusions, which were the opposite of those in the negative Ramspeck Report, and supported the AAF's request that the WASPs be militarized.

The members of the subcommittee…agree with General Arnold that the WASPs should be given military status and have the same responsibility as male pilots flying military airplanes, and, along with it, the same rights, privileges, and benefits to which such male pilots are entitled.

Unfortunately, the Appropriations Committee did not make the news, but the Ramspeck Report did. The public didn't know that the report they saw was filled with misinformation. The opinion pieces attacked the WASP Program as wasteful and worse. One suggested that General Arnold would do anything for Jacqueline Cochran and the WASPs because of Jackie's "windblown bob, smiling eyes and outdoor skin." Another wrote, "In colleges the smooth, good-looking gals can get A's without a lick of work; and in the armed services it may be that dimples have a devastating effect, even on generals." No evidence was presented to support either opinion piece.

WASPs continued to fly as the debate lingered on, mostly unaware of what was happening in Congress. Yet the negative publicity in newspapers around the country had a devastating effect on how military men or civilians saw us. Jackie suffered quietly for her cause, unwilling to seek out our support and intentionally keeping us out of the loop.

In mid-June, the entire House of Representatives began the debate on the bill. The Ramspeck Report was entered as fact-based evidence. Articles, editorials, and letters supporting the WASPs were ignored. We couldn't speak for ourselves because of the gag order. Those who opposed our militarization packed the Capitol's galleries, cheering as insults were thrown at us.

If only we could have testified, we could have named commanders who asked for WASPs on their bases. We would have described the respect combat pilots had for us. We would have mentioned Lieutenant Colonel Paul Tibbets, who had trusted WASPs to demonstrate the B-29 to hesitant male pilots. But we weren't invited to the hearings.

General Hap Arnold and the Secretary of War testified in support of the WASPs. Several members of Congress from the Military Affairs Committee, who knew more about the program than most other representatives, testified as well. They tried hard to reveal the truth. Their accurate statistics and expert opinions didn't help convince the representatives, who listened only to what they wanted to hear.

In the end, the bill to militarize the WASPs was defeated. Was there anything else anyone could do? General Hap Arnold and Jackie Cochran, after much thought and disappointment, decided there wasn't. In October, they sent us this devastating letter.

HEADQUARTERS OF THE ARMY AIR CORPS

WASHINGTON

3 November 1944

TO ALL MEMBERS OF THE WASP

Since the announcement of the WASP deactivation, a number of inquiries have been received from individual WASPs as to the opportunities for employment as pilots in various Allied countries.

I have no information at this time as to the need for women pilots by any foreign country. If a sufficient number of girls are interested in the Foreign Service, I shall be glad to get in touch with the various embassies and legations to determine whether any such need exists, and if so, whether they would be interested in using WASPs. Before doing so, however, it will be necessary to know how many women are interested.

If a need exists in any Allied countries for women pilots and you wish to volunteer, please write to me, with the following information.

A statement that you will serve in any Allied country that's willing to use your services.

For how long you could serve under contract conditions. It is probable that a minimum contract might run from eighteen months to two years.

Would you be willing to enlist in the military service of an Allied country, under whatever conditions enlistments are accepted?

Would you be willing to travel by ship to your assignment?

Salary required. It is likely that the salary will be much lower than that you now receive.

As you no doubt know, many personal hardships will be encountered in most foreign countries, which you have not had to face in your service with the WASPs. Before you make a decision, careful consideration should be given to all factors. Please be sure you are prepared to face such conditions before I recommend you to any of the various Governments.

Because of the volume of administrative work involved in the deactivation of the WASP, it will not be possible to undertake this placement until after 20 December 1944.

Jacqueline Cochran,
Director of Women Pilots

The WASPs were heartbroken. Betty Gillis was very angry, while Ann Baumgartner felt "incomplete" at not being able to continue to the war's end. We'd been told that our successes would lead to militarization. Instead we, who proved we could fly anything men could, were being sent home solely because of our gender. It felt like a funeral: a total shock and a tremendous loss.

Now, we would no longer be able to share our sorrows, fears and loneliness. We were losing more than our jobs; we were losing a close-knit community that we'd never have again.

Sadly, some former WASPs, especially those who had started with Nancy Love in Delaware, blamed Jackie for the program's demise. They said she had waited too long to push for militarization. They blamed her for ordering the women to stay quiet when they should have been defending themselves. They said she'd been pushy, stubborn, selfish and overconfident.

Those of us who trained in Texas strongly defended her. She'd lent many of us money to get to Avenger Field. She designed and paid for our silver wings at graduation. She'd been our mentor and our friend. The program would never have existed beyond a handful of pilots in Nancy Love's ferrying squadron.

We agreed she could be stubborn and pushy, but as Betty Jane Williams said, "If there was an obstacle, Jackie knew how to get around it. That kind of gutsiness and aggressiveness in a woman is not always admired. But, in a man, it's applauded."

Jackie Cochran had given the WASPs an opportunity to soar, and most of us wanted to keep soaring. Flying is an extremely hard habit to break.

TWENTY-TWO

The deactivation of the WASPs devastated us all. We were used to being very active "high-fliers", yet had been dropped like a load of bricks. I didn't know what depression was, but am willing to bet some of us are suffering from that now. Jackie has promised to come here soon to discuss all this with us, and we really need her.

I'm angry and sad and on top of everything else, my health problems continue. The doctor, who doesn't understand my crazy heart actions, has run more than a dozen tests. His conclusion: I'm okay but should visit the hospital every night for a check-up. I've pretty much stopped drinking coffee (just one cup for breakfast) and smoking. No more beer or any other alcoholic beverage. I don't even care. I go to bed around eight o'clock every night so I'm ready to fly again in the morning. What I won't do to keep flying!

My second ground school finishes on November 23rd and after that, who knows? We'll probably all be sent back home. I don't like the idea of returning to Macon to instruct. I'm going to look for something more interesting and concrete in another part of the country, or the world. I know a few people in Florida around Miami and will let them know I'm looking. I do want a place of my own.

"It's good to be with you again, my dear ladies. I want you to listen to me first, and then ask any questions after I finish. All of you know how much I care about you." Jackie was back, and for the first time in days, we were smiling.

"It wasn't easy being a director of women pilots. Not because of the basic premise of the program, but because of the hassle of breaking such new ground for women in what had been a highly prized corner of a man's world: flying. You proved the point about the excellence of female flyers, demonstrating that my training program, my operations, the WASPs—everything worked, and it worked extremely well."

She looked around the room, smiling back at us. "You were competent pilots in the ferry operation, flying the planes and personnel. Towing targets was a nasty job which you did well. You showed everyone that you could do as well or better than the men on tracking and search-light operations, simulated strafing, smoke laying and performing other chemical missions. You made engineering flights and radar calibration flights, and by doing all of this, you helped us meet a national emergency."

Jackie paused, searching our faces. "And now you are being deactivated. And you would like to know why, I'm sure."

We remained silent, waiting for her to continue.

"It seems the Army now has a surplus of male pilots who can do the jobs we've been doing. Because of that, they have let you go. But I won't…not until you find what you want to do next."

As I sat there listening, I was thinking about Australia.

Would I go there and work? Maybe she'd give us a better idea.

"My new plan, which I've just started, is to get some overseas duty for those of you who want it. Perhaps in Australia (*was she reading my mind?*) or even China. The plans are not definite yet, but I promise you I'm working as quickly as I can. It's the only way I know to thank you for believing in me."

One of the newer pilots timidly raised her hand. "Miss Cochran, why couldn't they just keep us on, even without military status? Isn't there enough work for the men and women?"

Jackie nodded. "There may be for a few weeks, but the war is coming to a close, and they are thinking ahead." She smiled. "And although you can't see it now, it is better for us to get you into other areas of aviation, where you'll find satisfaction and meet new goals."

That afternoon I understood what a true friend she has been to all of us. We can count on her to follow up with us, but we'll need to be flexible. Can I be that adaptable? Will my health allow it? Should I be looking for something more than "just making a living?" I'm not getting any younger, and I want to get into something that will give me more of a secure feeling financially. But I do know I have to continue in the field of aviation.

Jackie left us feeling stronger and more optimistic. Once again, she thanked us for our loyalty to her. We were uncertain as to whether we'd see her again, and that was difficult to admit.

After three years of service to my country, I'm out of a job. But my faith will keep me going, and I'm going to project and believe that a good opportunity will present itself to me. Patience…a word and practice I've always struggled with, has returned to haunt me. Daddy comes to mind often, and his words are uplifting. *Stay strong, my daughter. You will be fine.*

Hazel Jane Raines

The Air Transport Auxiliary Uniform, England 1942.
Courtesy of the Hawkins family.

Hazel instructing students in 1941. Courtesy of the Hawkins family.

Hazel in the Georgia Air Races and Show, 1940.

Vineville Methodist Church in Macon. Author photo.

Hazel's childhood home in Macon. Author photo.

Montreal, Canada flight training (Hazel in cockpit), 1943. Courtesy of the Hawkins family.

Hazel in English Spitfire.
Courtesy of the Hawkins family.

A.T.A. pilots (l to r) Sandoz,
Chapin, Souror, Raines.
Courtesy of the Hawkins family.

Mrs. Roosevelt inspecting A.T.A. pilots, England, October 26, 1942.
Hazel is second from the left. Courtesy of the Hawkins family.

Cliveden, home of Lady and
Lord Astor. Courtesy of the
Hawkins family.

Hazel with Lady Astor,
December 1942. Courtesy of
the Hawkins family.

2	24	Seafire	NM987	"			Chattis Hill — Luroughton		
2	24	Seafire	LR635	"			Luroughton — Lee on Solent		
2	25	Spitfire VIII	JF327	"			Eastleigh — Brize Norton		
2	25	Fairchild	EV289	"			—		
2	26	Spitfire VIII	JF334	"			Eastleigh — Brize Norton		
2	26	Spitfire V	AB391	"			Brize Norton — Swindon		
2	27	Seafire	NM934	"			Hamble — Luroughton		
2	27	Fairchild	HM174				Taxi		
				Summary for February, 1943		1-Spitfire			
				Unit : #15 F.P.P.		2-Hurricane			
				Date : February 28 1943		3- Master			
				Signature: Hazel Raines		4- Fairchild			
				Aircraft Types		5- T-Moth			
3	1	Spitfire II	EN490	"			Eastleigh — Cosford		
3	1	Spitfire V-B	AB366	"			Cosford — Swindon		
3	2	Spitfire IX	EN205	"			Hamble — Crashed Collingbourne Kingston		
				Summary for March 1943					
				Unit: #15 F.P.P.		1-Spitfire			
				Date: March 31, 1943					
				Signature: Hazel Raines					

GRAND TOTAL [Cols. (1) to (10)]
..................Hrs..................Mins.

TOTALS CARRIED FORWARD

Hazel's log on crash, 1943. Courtesy of the Hawkins family.

Hazel Jane Raines Spitfire Story

In March 1943 a Spitfire that was being delivered to a squadron had a total loss of power and crashed into Number 57 High Street in the centre of the Village. It was being flown by by the ATA pilot Hazel Jane Raines, who remarkably survived. Little did the Village realize just how remarkable this young lady who had just 'dropped in' was.

Courtesy of Collingbourne Kingston Parish Council.

Wesleyan Alumnae Instructs British Fliers

Hazel Raines, Conservatory '36, is now in England as an officer in the RAF, instructing fledgling fliers for combat duty.

Hazel first began her lessons in flying four years ago at the age of 20, and was one of the few women in the United States chosen as an instructor in the Civilian Pilot Training program. She was instructor at Ft. Lauderdale, Florida aviation school when a call came from Jacquelin Cochran, America's No. 1 woman pilot, asking if she would be available to join 24 other picked American aviatrixes as flight instructors in the Royal Air Force. She left in March for Canada and later the British Isles on her new commission.

The Wesleyan Alumnae, April 1942.

A Record of Achievement

- **25,000 women applied to be members of the WASP**
- **1,830 were accepted to the training program**
- **1,102 served as WASP**
- **12,652 planes were delivered by the WASP**
- **77 types of planes were flown by WASP**
- **60,000,000 miles were flown by WASP**
- **38 women died flying for their country**

Hazel (rt) with a fellow student.
Courtesy of the Hawkins family.

Hazel with an instructor.
Courtesy of the Hawkins
family.

Avenger Field, Sweetwater, Texas, 1944. Courtesy of the National
Archives Washington.

Flying to Avenger Field.
Courtesy of the National
Archives.

Daily physical training at Avenger
Field. Courtesy of the National
Archives.

Pauline Gower and Jackie
Cochran. Courtesy of the
Maidenhead Heritage Center..

Sunbathing at Avenger Field. Courtesy of the National Archives
Washington.

WASPs on the flight line. Courtesy of the National Archives Washington.

Jacqueline Cochrane and General Arnold. Courtesy of the National Archives Washington.

After their first solo flight, WASP trainees were thrown into the Wishing Well. Courtesy of the National Archives Washington.

WASPs classes taught by Jacqueline Cochran (in the middle with her hand up). Courtesy of the National Archives Washington.

Three WASPs waiting in the snow by their aircraft. Courtesy of the National Archives Washington.

Hazel and Crum in Rio with Christ the Redeemer statue, August 15, 1945. Courtesy of the Hawkins family.

Hazel in Brazil 1946. Courtesy of the Hawkins family.

Hazel in a Brazilian hearse, 1945. Courtesy of the Hawkins family.

Hazel, "Flying the Desk," 1952.
Courtesy of the Hawkins family.

Air Force uniform, 1953
Courtesy of the Hawkins family.

Maxwell Air Force Band, October 18, 1952. Courtesy of the
Hawkins family.

Hazel as a WAF recruiter, 1953. Courtesy of the Hawkins family.

Hazel Jane Raines, 1955.
Courtesy of the Hawkins family.

TWENTY-THREE

Jackie did indeed work her magic one more time. I'm learning Portuguese and enjoying it so much! I'll be moving to Sao Paulo, Brazil to teach aviation courses for local pilots. Irene Crum (I call her Crum), my best friend from Avenger Field, will be teaching there as well. We're taking a three-month immersion course here at the J.P. Riddle Company Instructors' School in Miami. Last week I gave a ten-minute speech in Portuguese. By the time I get to Brazil, I hope to be conversational and fluent (as much as three months can give you). I want to be able to conduct all my classes in Portuguese, even though most of the aviator students apparently speak fluent English.

I have written my family that we're in "high gear" now with our studies. This morning I gave a fifteen-minute speech in Portuguese about Getulio Vargas, the President of Brazil. My next speech is on Instrument Flying, a topic I chose, which will be harder for me, especially since the audience will be the Board of Directors. I have just one more speech next week, and the instructors will choose the topic.

Crum and I have been shopping for "professor out-fits" to wear at our school in Sao Paulo. To look profes-sorial, we've bought four suits and extra blouses. I'm already packing my trunk; we're only allowed sixty-five pounds of baggage. I'm almost there and I still need more shoes. Del and Harris (our Portuguese instructors) mentioned that we'll need hats as well—something I never considered. Apparently, there are some nice sport-type hats that look good and provide some shade from the sun.

I explained to Mother and my sisters about the slow mail delivery between Brazil and the States. I've become too accustomed to picking up the phone and talking to my family whenever I want. That would be incredibly expensive down there, so we're not even considering it. I learned that the postage fee for air mail is 20 cents, which isn't too bad.

I think we're leaving for Rio de Janeiro on August 8th. Del told us we will probably stay in Natal for several days before arriving in Rio. Crum and I now have a place to live in Sao Paulo, secured by a friend who studied with us here in Miami. We'll be staying in the Grao Para Hotel, where the rent will be half of what we paid in Miami.

I plan to continue writing a journal, as I did during my time in England and whenever I could in the U.S. Needless to say, I am ready, anxious and very excited to begin this new adventure.

August 15, 1945
Dearest Mother,
    Well, we made it! We're in Rio de Janeiro! We did stop in Natal for two days, will be here in Rio for three days, and then, off to Sao Paulo.

Rio is the capital of Brazil, so it is noisy and filled with many busy people. The rushing about is a bit unnerving after our quiet city/town lives, and will take some getting used to, but I imagine we'll find the same situation in Sao Paulo.

The colors of the flowers, bushes and trees are so bright and beautiful. And the architecture: I've never seen such beautiful buildings—very modernistic and so far ahead of anything I've ever seen in the States. You must come join me here and see it for yourself!

When we were in Natal, we practiced our Portuguese with the locals. We were sitting on a bench at the docks when two little boys offered to shine our shoes. Then a man walked over and invited us for a ride in a sailboat, so away we went…shoe-shine boys and all. Crum and I managed to make ourselves understood in their language, until the last moments of the trip, when the owner started speaking English to us. Very good English, in fact. We all shared a good chuckle and departed friends.

Yesterday afternoon we went to the cinema to watch an American movie. It was in English, with Portuguese subtitles flashed on the screen for the benefit of the locals. We discovered that is a great way to learn/understand Portuguese! After the movies we returned to our hotel, changed clothes and went out to a night club, where we ate, danced, practiced our Portuguese and watched others gamble. Oh, and the floor show was spectacular, with fancy colorful gowns and some interesting dance moves.

We and a few other customers also celebrated the end of the war! You know that Brazil sent some forces to

Europe that saw action in Italy, so we joined complete
strangers in the merriment. What are you doing to
celebrate at home? The American Consul has invited us
over to the Embassy this evening to celebrate the victory!
So I'm sure we will enjoy that before leaving for Sao
Paulo, and our new job.

Sending warm hugs,
Hazel Jane

TWENTY-FOUR

Starting a journal about my time here in Brazil has proved to be easier said than done. Between travels, moving in and out of three hotels and daily visits to the school where I will teach, I was just too tired at night to put pen to paper. And when we got up each morning, we rushed everywhere to keep up with our schedule. So, this is now the first chapter of my Brazilian diary.

I'm in Sao Paulo and staying in the Grao Para Hotel. Crum and I share a large room with a big bath, comfortable beds, and a small living room. Our accommodations were arranged by friends who arrived several weeks before us, also teachers at the Escola Técnica De Aviacao. We were welcomed with a large pot of beautiful orchids sitting on the table beside the sofa.

We haven't begun teaching yet, but have visited the school daily. There is a lot of class planning to complete before we begin to teach. They pick us up and bring us back in a school bus, so we don't need vehicles. We've been told that taxis and city buses are inexpensive if we need them.

But before I write any more about Sao Paulo, let me go back to our last day in Rio and describe my incredible impression of the beautiful Christ the Redeemer statue atop Mount Corcovado in Rio. Crum and I were determined to visit this Art Deco style monument before leaving Rio, and we're so happy we did!

We rode up in a cog-wheeled train, and then joined a guide at the foot of the statue. This was a perfect way to approach its history. I took notes as he spoke and will share what we learned. The statue stands ninety-eight feet tall, and its horizontally outstretched arms span ninety-two feet. It took nine years to build, beginning in 1922, and cost $250,000 U.S. This religious and cultural symbol warmly welcomes everyone to Rio de Janeiro.

Christ the Redeemer was actually built in France by the French sculptor Paul Landowski, who used reinforced concrete under an outer shell of six million soapstone tiles. It is rumored that workers who made these tiles often scribbled notes on the back, so this iconic landmark may be filled with hidden messages. Those tile pieces were shipped to Brazil and reassembled with reinforced concrete.

The statue stands majestically 2,300 feet above sea level. You can look down and see the entire city of Rio. Everything about this experience was so powerful it took my breath away!

I've seen high mountains in Georgia and other places, enjoyed them from above, but this was the first time I've felt like I was flying while standing on solid ground. The powerful combination of those welcoming outstretched arms, gazing at the beautiful city sprawled far below us, and imagining the horizon within arm's reach made it a breathtaking memory that reminded me of why I love to fly.

Until classes start, our days begin at 6:30 with coffee in the room. Then we go downstairs for "breakfast," or we can have it brought to our room, with more coffee. Crum eats the full breakfast, but it's too much for me: rolls with butter and jam, several types of local fruit (most of which

I have never eaten) and sweet breads. Later we eat our lunch at school, which is larger than American lunches, and in the evening, we go to a local restaurant for dinner.

The weather is nice, even though it is winter here. My suit keeps me comfortable during the day, with a light coat at night. What a relief to be out of the Miami heat and humidity!

Our new friends are Mr. and Mrs. del Junco, the parents of Del, our female instructor in Miami. They came by when we arrived and offered to help us in any way they could. If they are as nice and kind as their daughter, we'll be very blessed indeed.

Most people we've met speak some English, as well as Spanish, French, and/or German. I've learned that most Latin American countries teach several languages in school besides their native tongue. I wish the same were true in the U.S.

We were assigned to our departments today. Mine is Link and Instrument Flying, but I was also asked to go to the Basic Department and possibly teach a few weeks of Theory of Flight, because of my years in Aviation. I will enjoy teaching Flight Theory, and I know it will help me learn Portuguese.

Crum and I are still taking one-hour language classes daily in preparation for their "proficiency exam." To pass, we must write and speak the language very well. Our motivation is a salary raise, as well as feeling "fluent" in Portuguese. We've been told it usually takes from four to six months for foreigners to pass that test. So Crum and I have hired a private tutor to come to our hotel so we can take and pass the exam earlier!

I can't wait to share a "new attitude" with my mother and family. The more I study and learn, the more I get out of life, and I am learning to appreciate every moment. But my spelling, which is already terrible, is getting even worse. And sometimes I find myself talking backwards!

We are thinking about getting an apartment, so we can plan and prepare our own dinners. We come back to the hotel so tired every day, and we just want to undress and relax. We usually have to study as well.

The food here is delicious, especially the steaks. I order one almost every night. The chicken is also good, but not like the Southern fried chicken my mother cooks so well. Speaking of my mother, I miss her a lot.

I finally received my first letter from Mother. It's now September 2nd, and I have written her that I love it down here. I have never seen such beautiful and reasonably priced flowers. We're happy we can afford to buy them every week to brighten up our hotel room. We're still trying to find another place to live, but that's harder than we expected.

On Sundays we can sleep in, but last Sunday we were awakened by loud whooping noises outside our hotel. We first heard the drums and bugles, and assumed it was just a parade. Yep, they marched past our building until 11:30 a.m. It seemed that the Brazilian Army was marching in one direction, and then young boys, also with drums and bugles, in another direction. Apparently they were practicing for a parade, but their real objective must have been to see how much noise they could make. The boys were of every color, typical of the Brazilian people.

We haven't begun teaching our classes, but now we're observing them. Due to a shortage of instructors, I was asked to start teaching Theory of Flight courses. I've never taught ground school, so this should be fun and a little uncomfortable. I will have a class of about twenty boys and two girls and will explain how an airplane flies, in Portuguese. I tried that last week and think I did rather well.

The school offers sightseeing trips every weekend and covers the expenses, so Crum and I finally took advantage of this and went to "Campos do Jordao." It was a six-hour trip, and I have never had such a ride! The roads were almost all dirt and bumpy, so the driver had to navigate one dangerous curve after another. I finally forced myself to relax, and in the end, we made it just fine.

We arrived at the Grande Hotel at the Campos do Jordao about 10 p.m., and made a beeline for the warmth of the huge fireplace in the lobby. Then everyone went to their rooms to wash off the layers of dirt. We came back downstairs for dinner, which I didn't expect. I thought I couldn't possibly eat that late, but of course I did: seven delicious courses, almost every one of which I finished.

The next morning seven of us went horseback riding through the mountains. I saw birds and flowers I never knew existed. While our horses enjoyed a long drink at a creek, we had a good stretch and explored. It was so beautiful. After another good meal at the hotel, we spent the afternoon relaxing on the terrace, soaking up warm sunshine and playing cards.

After a late dinner, we danced to the music of a small local orchestra, and got to know people from different parts of Brazil. I slept in the next day, and couldn't even think about riding horses again since I was still sore. Two other instructors stayed with me. We sat on the porch, reading, resting and talking.

I have a cold now, probably due to the chilly weather. There are four or five warm hours in the middle of the day, but the daily changes in temperature don't suit me. Nose drops have been helpful. I am also taking vitamin shots at the local pharmacy.

One instructor at the school in the Theory of Flight department has gone to Rio, so I'm taking his classes for a week or two. I like the work and only hope my Portuguese is good enough to teach them properly.

I miss being outdoors and flying, so I trust the flight school will get set up soon. Sometimes I remember my time in England and all the free time we had to fly. Here we're just going through the same routines every day. And my heart pushes me to *get out and fly*!

TWENTY-FIVE

I have a funny anecdote to share. I often visit the local pharmacy to get a Vitamin B shot, and yesterday I decided to buy some Sodium Perborate to use as a mouthwash. It also helps keep teeth white. When I asked the pharmacist for it, he frowned so I thought I had been misunderstood.

"I'm so sorry, Miss," he said in English. "That substance is controlled by the Minister of War because it is highly explosive. I cannot sell it to you."

"So I can't buy it anywhere in Brazil?" I asked him, confused.

He shook his head. "Not without official permission, which is very difficult to obtain."

I was determined, so I went to the doctor at my school and in my best Portuguese, explained my predicament.

His face lit up. "Oh yes, I know exactly what you want," he smiled, walking toward the back.

I paid and took the package to my hotel room. As I unwrapped it I paused, scowled, and then burst into laughter. He had given me cough syrup instead of mouthwash. Maybe I need to work harder on my Portuguese.

Crum discovered a little shop down the street where they make exquisite dolls. I've decided to order some for my nieces, and maybe even one for me since they're so pretty. You just tell them in the shop which doll you would like, the size you want, and they make it there! These are nice, inexpensive gifts for girls of all ages.

Americans and other foreigners love to purchase an incredible variety of leather goods made locally. Beautiful wallets and pocketbooks only cost around $10.00 U.S. I'm thinking of taking some to Mother and my sisters. They come in all colors of pigskin, calfskin, alligator and even snakeskin. I've bought myself a good-looking pair of alligator shoes, which I'll describe to my family and ask what colors they may like. This could be difficult though, since they measure your feet and make them to your exact size.

I've met a very nice man named Donald Pettigrew, originally from upstate New York. He's been living here for six years and works for Firestone. I actually met him during that weekend trip to Campos do Jordao, when he joined us on Saturday night for dinner and dancing. He's a good dancer, slightly taller than me, has light brown hair and hazel eyes, is courteous and has done many interesting things in his life.

We've been out to dinner twice and went dancing one other time. I enjoy spending evenings with him. I don't think either of us is looking for a permanent relationship, but it is relaxing and fun to share a nice afternoon or evening together.

My Theory of Flight classes continue but I'm still not flying, which is very frustrating. My students are energetic and funny, and understand my Portuguese well enough to ask questions. Sometimes I explain the answers in English, which most of them usually understand, and other times I ask for a translator. We use our hands a lot to speak Portuguese (like the Italians and Spaniards.) I believe if someone were to tie mine behind me, I couldn't say a word.

Crum and I have looked for apartments to rent, but the ones with two bedrooms are just too expensive. And we'd probably need a maid to clean up after us, since we're too busy to do much housekeeping. Maids are also hard to find. We really want to cook our own food, but the cleaning would probably fall on my shoulders because Crum isn't as tidy as I am, and we both get lazy when we're tired. So, here we will stay for the time being. I'm thinking about maybe renting a smaller single room in the hotel.

The del Juncos have invited us to dinner this weekend. They also insisted that I invite Donald, since I had already made plans to see him. They continue to send us fruit and flowers and they check in on us frequently.

I missed joining them for lunch several weeks ago because I had a bad ear infection. The school doctor has been treating it every day, and it's finally better. But I'm always wondering which health issue will plague me next.

Sunday Morning
October 7, 1945
Dearest Mother,

I enjoyed receiving your letter yesterday. It's so nice when they arrive on Saturday when I'm home. And thanks for answering all my questions. I agree with you about the dolls, and just want you to know that all the pocketbooks are lined with soft leather.

Please don't worry about the news you may be hearing, because we are safe and so is this country. We thought we might have a little excitement this week, but we didn't. As you know, the politics here are very different from ours at home—not as democratic, and this is certainly not a government by the people. Now they have begun their political campaigns and rallies for the upcoming election on December 2nd.

At school yesterday, the directors told us to prepare at least three days' supply of food. They said if something happened we wouldn't be able to leave the hotel. The politicians had a big meeting here in Sao Paulo, and the school thought there might be trouble. But nothing happened. And please know that we aren't worried about our safety, because the American Consul is just behind our hotel, and they will look after us.

Did I write you about the lovely lunch we enjoyed at the house of our friends the del Juncos? They live in a charming old home about seven miles outside the city, with lots of fruit trees and vegetables growing in the garden, and chickens, ducks, two dogs, a horse, several cats and some bunnies roaming the yard. We had such a nice time. My friend Donald joined us and enjoyed himself. Of course, having lived here for six years or so, his Portuguese is impressive, but the del Juncos speak fluent English too, so we mostly conversed in English.

Time down here seems to be flying. My contracted year's stay will be ending in August of next year, and I must decide whether I'll stay longer. As it is, Christmas is just around the corner. I will miss spending it at home with you, but am pretty sure there will be many festive activities here to keep us busy.

I think prices are going up now because of the season, or maybe the upcoming elections? Everything suddenly seems to be more expensive.

Tomorrow is another holiday, so we don't have school. They celebrate what they call "Wings Day", or something like that. These people have a holiday at the drop of a hat. Of course we don't mind, but I wonder if these classes I'm teaching will ever end. The money is very good, but we all know that money isn't everything.

I used to ask school officials when we instructors could fly. I no longer ask. As much as I like teaching others to fly, I need to get up into the air again. It's in my bloodstream. Yet, it doesn't seem to be part of the plan for us; at least, not for now.

Sending lots of love,
Hazel Jane

TWENTY-SIX

I've been feeling sorry for myself because I'm not flying, and now this. I guess God knew all along that my ear would be acting up again. When the del Juncos heard about it, they took me to see another ear specialist. After a lot of tests he gave me a new medication, which has already helped. He believes he can save the hearing in my right ear. So, even if I were cleared to fly, I couldn't go until this problem is settled.

All of us wonder what will happen to American instructors now that President Vargas has been forced to resign by the military leaders. School has been closed for almost a week, so I have had time to read and discuss this state of affairs with local friends.

Donald and the del Juncos have lived here for years (Donald was living and working here during the war) and are the most unbiased sources I could find to explain to me why President Vargas was forced to resign. They clarified that the people of Brazil wanted a democracy, and although their government defended it abroad, the authoritarian policies decreed by Vargas made it impractical. The political movements and democratic demonstrations in our streets forced the president to abolish censorship in 1945, release many political prisoners, and allow the reformation of other parties, including the Brazilian Communist Party.

"Mr. del Junco, did you say the Brazilian Communist Party supports President Vargas?" I wondered.

"Yes, it has been supporting him since Moscow directed it to."

"Then why does the president try to advocate democracy?"

Donald spoke up. "I think it's a matter of whom you ask. You know that Bishop Duarte Costa, and the Catholic Church in general, are outspoken critics of the President's regime, although his nickname is 'Father to the poor.' Some say the Vatican has a relationship with fascist regimes and that Rome even aided and abetted Hitler."

Mrs. del Junco understood my bewilderment. "Hazel, many rumors have surfaced, but nobody really knows the whole story. Most of what is happening doesn't affect us directly. For example, President Vargas established the Brazilian Labor Party to gain the support of the urban workers, who still support him. Then he added the *Additional Act* to our Constitution, providing a 90-day period during which a time and date for elections would be designated."

"So that's why we've had all this time off," I teased. "And that ninety days is up less than three weeks from now."

"So his resignation really means very little," added Mr. del Junco. Acting President José Linhares will do nothing until the December 2nd election, when a new president will be voted in."

"And President Vargas will not run?"

Donald shook his head. "No, Hazel. He has already chosen Eurico Gaspar Dutra, his friend, to replace him on the ballot. Rumor says Vargas now wants to run for the Senate." I was surprised at Donald's extensive knowledge of Brazilian politics.

Our lives continued moving forward slowly, with few classes to teach because of the many holidays. Nevertheless, some new girls from Coral Gables, Florida, joined us. Poor things: they felt as confused as we were when we arrived. We helped them order lunch from the Portuguese menu at school, and suggested they get Portuguese tutors to prepare for classroom teaching.

All the seasons here are backwards. When it's spring in the United States, it's fall here. So far, the weather hasn't been too hot. Just a lot of rain. So we're making the best of it and enjoying the benefits, such as the abundance of colorful flowers.

With so many different varieties of flowers, and often receiving fresh bouquets from the del Juncos and Donald too, we've wrapped up a huge water bucket in red and green cellophane paper to use as a vase. It looks very Christmassy. The new flower that we place in it is bright red and called "Beco de Papagaio", which means Parrot's Beak. It's so big it can't fit into normal vases; hence, the large water bucket. I guess this will be our only Christmas decoration this year, but we don't need anything more to liven up our apartment.

Breaking News: we are getting fitted for uniforms. At least this will keep my lovely dress suits in better condition. The uniforms are tan, like khaki but with better material. We'll get them on Dec. 1st, the day before the elections are held.

Several American women instructors are having a luncheon at the Jockey Club and have invited us to join them. We've never been there but have heard it's a lovely place with delicious food. They'll have horse races that afternoon and I plan to place a few bets.

I miss Mother so much and had hoped she could visit, but I won't take any chances until after the elections. By then, perhaps I'll have found an apartment where we could cook and be more comfortable. They just told me the single hotel room I wanted will be ready in a week. It's on the seventh floor, and Crum is also pleased that she'll soon have this space to herself. She's been a grand person to live with, but I need more independence, and happily, she feels the same way.

I believe my gloomy mood these days reflects the uncertainty of my future and the insecurity of Brazil's government leading up to this election. But it's probably really about the simple reality that I'm not doing what I love the most: flying. My hope and prayer is that we'll be assigned to airplanes soon, but I don't think anything will happen until the elections are over. And then, only God knows.

TWENTY-SEVEN

It's Election Day evening, December 2, 1945, and everything is quiet in the city. We stayed inside the hotel all day, catching up on letter writing, reading, and talking to friends who stopped by to visit. Donald loves to cook and came over to cook a steak dinner for the three of us.

With very little drama, it appears that Eurico Gaspar Dutra of the Social Democratic Party has won the presidency. He was President Vargas's hand-picked choice. Vargas demonstrated his popular support by winning the Senate vote. Women vote here as well (since 1932), but the election is not discussed much. My Portuguese female friends told me they had voted.

I will be moving to the seventh floor of this hotel tomorrow, and I am ready to live alone. Crum and I have been invited by a group of instructors from our school to travel to Argentina over the holidays. We thanked them but decided it might be more fun to fly over to Rio and join my aviator friend Sissy, who is coming down from the U.S. to meet us there. That will be our unconventional Christmas holiday.

"While you girls are enjoying Rio, I've decided to go back home to spend Christmas with my family," Donald told me yesterday. He has seemed restless and homesick lately, and has not been back to the States in over a year.

"Your family will be so happy to see you," I smiled, squeezing his hand.

Donald nodded, giving me a tired smile in response. "Hazel, when will you go home for a visit?"

I shook my head. "I don't know. So much of my life has been about trying to control exactly where I was headed. I'm feeling I should just let life come at me; let the best and the worst things happen naturally."

He answered slowly. "Nobody knows what's ahead. Take nothing for granted, but be willing to dare anything, everything." He stretched his long legs and stood up, pulling me to my feet as well. "And then, let it go."

I laughed. "How did you get so smart?"

"T.S. Elliot taught me. *'Teach us to care and not to care. Teach us to be still.'*"

We three girls had our non-conventional Christmas after all. A friend who decided to visit relatives in Rio kindly included us in her plans. Sara Harrison is married to a local doctor and teaches with Crum and me. When she heard we would be spending Christmas in the capital, she invited us to her aunt's home for a typical Brazilian Christmas dinner.

Brazilian Christmas traditions come from Portugal, which ruled Brazil for centuries. Like the Mexican Posadas, Brazilian Christmas plays—Os Pastores—are presented every night for several weeks before Christmas. We were thrilled to see two of them: one in Sao Paulo and another one in Rio. The shepherds travel to celebrate baby Jesus's birth, knocking on doors to be invited to the manger. In the Brazilian tradition, there is also a shepherdess and a woman who tries to steal the baby.

We joined Sarah's family in a lovely Catholic Church for the Christmas Eve Midnight Mass, which finished at 1 a.m., and was followed by fireworks. Sara's family decided it would be better for us to sleep in and then enjoy Christmas dinner with them at 3 p.m. on Christmas Day.

Like in our country, the most popular Christmas song is "Noite Feliz" (Silent Night). We sang along in English and fit right in. Then they told us about an end-of-year tradition: *the "13th" salary.* In December, citizens are paid twice their normal salary in order to boost the economy around Christmas. This has been going on for decades, and they don't even question that other countries might not do that. We giggled and wondered aloud if we'd return to school to find our *"13th"* salary.

Our Christmas lunch was delicious! We ate pork, turkey, salads, vegetables and fresh and dried fruits. Everything is served with rice cooked with raisins and a spoonful of "farofa" (seasoned manioc flour). Our desserts were panettone (a soft Italian bread loaf filled with dried fruit), sweet rebanadas, and tropical fruits and ice cream. It was a feast lasting over two hours, filled with laughter and cheer. How I appreciate the graciousness of our Brazilian friends!

March 8, 1946

Dearest Mother,

We are boiling our drinking water now because there were two hundred new cases of typhoid in this city last week. I don't think we have to worry, because we had shots for typhoid, tetanus, and a dozen other tropical diseases before we came down here. We also took them in England, and again with the WASPs, and then just to be on the safe side, they gave us booster shots in Miami. So please do NOT worry when you read the health reports about Sao Paulo.

Speaking of health, I have been taking calcium and iron shots from an English doctor I'm seeing. He said I was okay in every way, but could use more fresh air and sunshine, so I'm following his orders. I traveled to Serra Negra with Crum at the end of February, where we both rested up and relaxed.

Then we returned to Sao Paulo February 27th, and took off on March 1st for Rio. Imagine me frolicking with the locals and tourists during "Carnaval"—the proper spelling in Portuguese! The people dressed in the most outrageous costumes, some very beautiful, and danced in the streets night and day for three days! Oh Mother, I have never had such a good time at a party!

They have parades filled with revelers, floats and adornments from many Samba schools. These schools are collaborations of neighbors who attend Carnaval together. They dance in elaborate costumes that usually tell a story. I never could figure out the stories, but that didn't matter.

These Carnaval celebrations date back to the 1650s, where feasts were organized to honor Greek wine gods. In 1840, the first Rio masquerade took place, and they told us that the polka and waltzes were popular dances then.

In 1888, Princess Isabel of Branance abolished slavery in Brazil. Finally the Afro-Brazilians were able to participate and transform the original massive masquerade to its present form, including the African traditions of masks, parades and most importantly, rhythm, which redefined the event. These former slaves near Rio brought African and Portuguese-Brazilian traditions together and developed the musical genre of the "Samba." In 1917, the Samba officially became the traditional music of Carnaval.

We participated in street festivals, without having to purchase tickets. Since everyone was dancing everywhere, we quickly got into the spirit of the party, and loved watching the obvious joy radiating from their faces.

We left Rio on March 5th to return to Sao Paulo, but couldn't land here because of bad weather. The pilot flew us all to the city of Bauru, fifty miles west, in the interior. We had a wonderful time in Bauru! It was the last day of Carnaval, and Pan American Airlines organized a party at one of the clubs and invited us all. How fun it was dancing the Samba (where we now felt like pros) and making merry once again!

I missed you and my sisters and their families. I really wished y'all could have joined us, either in Bauru or in

Rio. Please promise me that we'll experience this together one day. And, who knew that one bad weather day could offer us so much fun?

Soon winter will be here. We've been without hot water in our hotel for almost a week. I have a little alcohol burner where I can heat a certain amount of water, but definitely not enough to take a good bath. Oh, the people and the things I miss from home!

Sending love to the family,
Your Hazel Jane

TWENTY-EIGHT

I turned thirty years old yesterday (April 21st) and celebrated it at a lake cottage near Sao Paulo. Two dear
friends have been here with me for a week: Crum and
Dotty, and Donald arrived Friday afternoon for the weekend. We've truly enjoyed sunbathing, fishing, boating,
swimming, and eating! I finally learned how to use the
wood stove, and have been cooking fried chicken for days.
I'll never get it to taste as good as Mother's, but my friends
seem to like it.

On Friday night we put together a Southern fiesta.
Besides fried chicken, I made corn- bread, collard greens,
macaroni and cheese, and even sweet tea. My other friends
cooked up a storm as well, and Donald brought beverages,
plus flowers, and several desserts, including a birthday
cake from my favorite neighborhood bakery.

Seeing Donald again, so generous and supportive,
stirred up questions I had never asked myself before. Did
I want to try and make a long-distance relationship grow
deeper? And was he the right person for me to do that
with? The only relationships I'd ever cared about in the
past had been with my family, my career, my teammates,
and airplanes. Where might Donald fit into that future?

As he raised a toast, Donald's eyes flickered over my
face, almost nostalgically. I sensed he might be having the

same kind of practical doubts that I had. I just wanted to make these hours together special and memorable.

We sang, danced, and sat around the fire sharing childhood stories. Dotty remembered some great ghost stories, and we all had a good scare over them.

The rented vacation cottage is just across the lake from a little Swiss inn, and to my total surprise, Crum and the others threw me a birthday party there. The inn was already hosting a dance to celebrate the end of Lent, so most of the attendees came dressed in native Swiss costumes. Some dancing was Swiss style, and we gamely joined in. Two of the hosts gave exhibition dances—entertaining and beautifully performed.

The owner of the inn offered me a lovely cake and a small plaque.

"Oh, my goodness," I told him, surprised and delighted. "This is so beautiful! And the cake as well! You shouldn't have done this!"

His bright smile was contagious. "Thank you, Miss Hazel, and a very Happy Birthday to you!"

"Did you paint this Swiss mountain scene? It looks so much like where we are!"

He beamed as he folded the wrapping paper. "It is indeed this mountain and my inn. If you wish, I will paint you another one, so you will have a pair."

I felt so happy. Maybe thirty won't be so bad after all. If only I could have been surrounded by family as well as friends. But perhaps next year? I know then I'll be back home, with a business of my own, and independent. But the most important part of next year's birthday will be flying again! I get excited just thinking about it.

I wondered why the possibility of seeing Donald in the future seemed to fade more with every thought of flying again.

I haven't told my family yet, and have only discussed this idea with Crum and Donald. My friend Sissy and I want to go into some sort of business in Oklahoma City after I return. It was her idea, but I agreed, mostly because it will take me back to aviation. There's a big municipal field in Oklahoma City now opened to private aviation. She's looking for a hangar and office space there, and we would find several planes to rent out. We'd also like to offer a rental car service for pilots and airline passengers who would need a vehicle for a few days.

Sissy tells me this is happening at some of the larger airports all over the country. She's done some research and doesn't think it will require a large initial investment. The biggest problem will be finding the equipment, especially the cars. If we start up this business and later have to get out of it, we'd simply sell the equipment.

I'm thinking about writing to Frankie's husband Reginald and asking his opinion, and if he agrees, he could buy two new Fords for us to start with. He does a lot of business with several automobile dealers in Macon, and hopefully we could have the cars by August. One of my WASP friends in California started the same service in an airport out there, and she says it's going great. Of course, once I let Reginald into the plan, I'll need to tell my other family members, and I hope Mother doesn't come up with reasons not to start up a new business.

I believe it will be a good deal for us, and I'm anxious to get started. I definitely want to settle down in the States when I return. I've had enough of traveling for a while. Crum and I got offers to go to China, but I said "No, thank you." I want to go home. Besides, I'd have to start studying Chinese, and I'm so tired of going to school. I need to rest for a while.

"Hazel, have you thought about Donald and what he might do when you leave?" Crum doesn't mince words, which I appreciate.

I looked up from the table. "Well, he's also thinking about leaving. His contract is up in about six months."

"Hmm, and let me guess. He wants to move to Oklahoma, too?" Her grin softened the moment.

"No, he will go back to New York. We will probably try to keep our relationship going in some form. Friendship doesn't really die, even over long distance."

"And the fact that you fly is an extra bonus to get together, right?"

I sent her a grateful smile. "Life has its twists and turns. I'm so happy you and I will always find each other. I'll hate to be missing both of you, but I know it won't be forever."

We stepped outside. The late afternoon light painted the mellow landscape with rare layers of shimmering gold.

"Oh, how I wish we could just climb up into these colors, don't you, Crum? I really miss the sky, and losing myself in its beauty."

She grinned. "You've told me several times that the sky is your home. Soon, you'll be returning to your home."

TWENTY-NINE

After much thought and researching, I decided to return home as soon as possible to prepare for a big Aviation Convention in Oklahoma in late October. Sissy and I need to be open for business before then. I'll have to work extra hard to meet people, because I'm not known yet in Oklahoma City. Unfortunately, I've lost contact with people in the aviation industry, having been away from civilian flying for the past five years.

But I'm excited to begin this new adventure, as is Sissy. I've decided not to wait until my contract expires in August. I resigned early this morning, effective July 1st. I was here for only eleven months, but I think my decision to move on was wise. I will return to Macon on July 5th, stay with my family for two weeks, and then go to Oklahoma City to open the new business.

I finally admitted to Mother in a letter that I haven't been happy these last several months, sitting on the ground teaching, when I wanted to be flying. Of course I've enjoyed my time here, made some wonderful friendships, and learned basic Portuguese, so I'm not complaining. But flying is my life, and we had no opportunities to fly in Brazil. So no regrets about returning one month early, because I believe it's in my best interest.

It's been almost two months since I put pen to paper, and a lot has happened in the United States. I spent two happy fun-filled weeks with my family in Macon, then flew to Oklahoma City to meet Sissy. We've been working with a friend of hers, Mr. Sieber, who helped us submit our aviation business proposal to the City Council. It was accepted, but then postponed for two weeks, until after City, County and State elections.

We're also considering the aircraft parts business. Mr. Sieber says he could fix us up in a nice store and warehouse with an office in one of the buildings next to his hotel.

"Sissy, why is Mr. Sieber taking such an interest in our business?" I wondered aloud.

She shrugged. "He and my parents have been friends for years, and he considers me another daughter," she said.

"It just seems a little odd that he's so concerned that we make it."

"Yesterday he told me he just wants to help us get off to a good start."

"Well," I insisted, "he told me that he wanted to put me up in a business where I would not have to work so hard. I guess he has a lot of confidence in us." I didn't tell her that his intense interest made me a little uncomfortable.

And in the end, neither venture was meant to be. Politics and changes to the economy made them both too complicated to work out. But I already knew how tricky starting a business could be.

In a way, being a pilot is like running a business. It isn't my plane, but once I step into the cockpit I am responsible for everything. A good business owner begins his day by making sure everything's in good working order, just as I check my plane's control panel and moving parts. Daddy taught me "how to take care of business".

As a grade school student, I learned about business from Mr. Nichols at his variety store. There was always something to straighten up or dust off. I soon got good at sweeping the aisles, straightening the displays, winding up his old wall clock with a key, and piling candy bars in little pyramids in the window. My "payment" would be a Moon Pie or Goo Cluster, popular Southern sweets.

Another idea came to me one afternoon. There's a new type of coin-operated radio on the market. These radios are made in Houston, Texas, for hotels and tourist courts. They operate for two hours when a quarter goes into the slot. I called the man from the company, and he agreed to come here and meet me. We got along great, and I bought the franchise to distribute these radios in western Oklahoma.

I'll be the distributor and will need to find operators in different sections of my territory. The radios sell for $63.15 to hotels and courts. I'll pay $50.00 for them. Or, if they just want to rent them, I'll do that on a percentage basis. I'll give hotels and courts 32% or 8 cents out of each quarter dropped in the slot. After deducting taxes, I will make 14 cents out of each quarter. I hope to make at least one quarter daily.

Sissy found another job in a city several hours away, so now I'm on my own. Mr. and Mrs. Sieber have agreed to let me install fifty radios in their hotel. I think I can either sell or rent at least 1500 radios within the next year.

Because I'm working by myself, it will be more work than I expected. But I think eventually I'll have a nice income.

I will have to travel a lot, and I hope I'm ready for that. My first order for five hundred radios will be installed in three different towns in southern Oklahoma—just as soon as I can deliver them. But I need to get a car, and no one can promise me one before the first of the year, which is a real problem.

I am in contact with Donald and Crum, and I miss them both. They've encouraged me to follow my dreams, but these are not my dreams. I want to fly again…not just for a while, but for a living. Fortunately, I've been able to fly a few times already, but my new life is taking a whole different turn and eating up most of my time.

I've also been in contact with Jackie Cochran. She brought me up to date on some friends from our flying days. She sounded somewhat despondent on the telephone.

"Most of the girls went home to anonymity, to changed marriages, and to a world that did not understand why they became so quiet when war stories were brought up. You, Hazel, continued to learn and have adventures. You were one of the fortunate ones."

I told her about trying to start up a business, and confessed that my heart was not in it. "If this radio business doesn't pan out, I will probably become a flight instructor somewhere in Oklahoma."

She liked that idea. "Stay close to aviation, my dear. You'll have another opportunity in that field. You're too good a pilot to stay grounded."

I asked her what she was doing. "Mostly, I'm resting and living off our wealth," she laughed lightly. "You must know that I'm not well-liked by many in the aviation world."

"No, I don't believe that!"

"Oh Hazel, so many people dislike those who succeed," she answered. "They call me a braggart, a liar, an enemy, a control freak and much worse. You've been away and missed a lot of this, but it's been disconcerting and vicious."

There was a long silence until I found the right words. "Jackie, to those of us who worked with you, you are the best. You fought for us, you cared about us, and you even found us jobs after the war."

"Thank you, Hazel," she said quietly. "You always were one of the sweetest, smartest girls I ever knew."

"Jackie, please keep in touch, and one day I'll surprise you with a visit. Or better yet, you come to me and I'll take you to lunch."

I loved the sound of her laughter. "You've got it, Hazel. I'll show up when you least expect it. Good luck with your radio business, and stay close to the planes. My next plan is to break the world speed record for women. Keep in touch, and I'll see you in the air!"

THIRTY

I stopped journaling for several years. I'm not really sure why, but probably because my "adventures" during this time were nothing like those of the past, and I had no motivation to write about them. My radio business was short-lived, (six months total) so I quickly signed up to teach aviation in Oklahoma. I was able to fly a lot during that time: the one pleasure that brightened my days and kept me optimistic.

My good news is that I've stayed active in women's aviation organizations. I collected some brochures and just came across one about the *Women's Aviation Convention*, sponsored by the *Texas Ninety Niners* on February 8-9, 1947. Nancy Love and I were featured speakers. It was great spending time with her, the former director of the WAFS, whom I had gotten to know back in England. She had always been so nice to all of us.

My topic for the convention was "Flying in Three Countries". Mother told me it was a great speech, and it was so special having her in the audience as I relived my flying adventures.

I loved attending air shows, demonstrations or practices in our area. The wartime newsreels, followed by the return of many pilots from overseas hungry to relive their aviation experiences, led to a dramatic surge in the public desire to be around aviators and their planes.

Most avid flight fans at these events were boys or men, but when audiences included women, sometimes I would be pointed out by fellow aviators and find myself surrounded by housewives and children, full of questions. They told me that their dreams of being airborne matched my real-life memories.

And my memories often returned to the excitement of being airborne: that instant when a plane's wheels lift off the runway, or how your stomach slides during a steep turn, or how hundreds of complex machine pieces work together to magically lift you toward the Heavens.

In December of 1948, I participated in the *Flying Day Contest*. Here is a passage from a WASP newspaper article two years later.

> The girl with the most flying hours was Hazel Raines and her award was a handsome ladies' wrist watch, donated by Davison's Jewelry Store in Los Angeles.
>
> She was also a WASP honor representative in the memorial service for the 38 WASPs who lost their lives in World War II. This service was held at the third Annual Convention Order of Fifinella (September 15-18, 1948) in Glendale, California. The Order of Fifinella was the peacetime organization composed of former members of the WASPs. Hazel was the national president of this elite group in 1950.

Our organization was described in an article in the *Atlanta Journal and Constitution Magazine* dated December 17,

1950. Mention was made of the silver dollar that Mother and Daddy had given me thirteen years earlier, when I earned my pilot's license. I carry it with me always; not only when I fly, but also as my reminder that God alone has guided my life. The article was written by Mary Holtzclaw, a journalist who had written several articles about me during my flying career. Her words were kind and thoughtful.

> When the WASPs were deactivated about five years ago, they started the peace-time organization called "The Order of Fifinella." Hazel's pretty dimples show when she talks about it. "You know," she says, "all of us in the Air Force believe in gremlins. Some of them are bad gremlins that hop up and down on the wings, or pour water in your fuel, or shriek like banshees. But Fifinella is a good gremlin. She was designed by Walt Disney for just us." The female gremlin is pictured on the emblem Hazel wears—a pretty little elf seated atop a plane, with her hair blowing in the wind.
>
> She's good luck too—but not as good as that silver dollar that has gone with Hazel on every flight since her first one 13 years ago. "Each time I take to the air," she says, "I get that silver dollar from my pocket and finger the words, 'In God We Trust.' Those are great words, and flyers have to believe them."

In September of 1949, I received a Reserve commission of 2nd Lt, USAFR. With that recognition, I could participate in the Organized Reserve Program at Lackland Air Force Base in San Antonio, Texas, during May of 1950. Guerrilla attacks along the 38th parallel between North and South Korea had begun. On June 25, 1950, North Korean Communist troops invaded South Korea, and war was declared.

Since the United Nations Charter, signed in 1945, had outlawed aggressive attacks, the U.N. asked member countries to aid South Korea. This conflict might give me an opportunity to serve my country! So I decided to write directly to the Director of the Women in the Air Force.

Yukon, Oklahoma
May 17, 1950
Colonel Geraldine P. May Director
Women in the Air Force
Pentagon Building Washington, D.C.

Dear Colonel May:
*   This letter may be an unpardonable course of action as well as a breach of "Channel" procedure, but I have exhausted every other known effort in an attempt to apply for Extended Active Duty. Will you be kind enough to give consideration to the following facts relative to my situation?*
*   On 15 September, 1949, I received a Reserve Commission of 2nd Lt., USAFR, Authority of appointment—AFL 35-103 B dated 17 November 1948. As of 21 February 1950, I was attached to Hg & Hg Sq., 3700th WAF Training Group, Lackland Air Force Base and given a DySSN 2520. In March I reported to this base*

for fifteen days Active Duty Training as well as twelve periods of "On-the-Job" training as assistant Group Training Officer.

The training I received while at Lackland has led me to believe there must a place for me in your WAF Program. My experiences have been broad due to affiliated service with the RAF in England, 1942-1943, fourteen months as a member of the WASPs, and one year as a Ground School Instructor for the Brazilian Air Ministry in Sao Paulo, Brazil. For the past fourteen years I have been working with men and women in a training and supervisory capacity.

While at Lackland, I learned they need additional Training Officers. I am confident in my interest, desire and ability to work with the WAF Program in this capacity. Accordingly, I applied for Extended Active Duty through the 12th Air Force, Brooks Field on 11 April 1950.

At the same time, I wrote to Major Marjorie Hunt, Continental Air Command, asking her for support of my application. Major Hunt wrote that my request for active duty has not yet been received. She thought they might be holding my application on file at the 12th Air Force because I do not have a critical "Military Operation Specialty."

Never having been service connected, a MOS was automatically "assigned" to me without considering my qualifications or past working experience. I believe I am qualified for a critical MOS that would support justification for my recall to the WAF Program or in our Air Forces.

While I appreciate how busy you must be, I hope you will support this recall request. Thank you very much in advance.

I understand you plan to be in San Antonio in June. If you could spare me a few minutes, I would be glad to drive down for an interview.

Sincerely,
Hazel J. Raines
2nd LT USAFR AL-1855750
Yukon, Oklahoma

THIRTY-ONE

An article in *The Atlanta Journal* on December 17,
1950 reported the thrilling news: *Georgia's Flying
Lady is the first WAF Reservist in the nation to be
returned to active duty on a mobilization assignment.*

I had been sitting on pins and needles as I waited to
learn the outcome of my bold letter. When the official
announcement came, I was shocked and overjoyed! It
seemed I wouldn't need to ask Jackie for help this time.

My answer came relatively soon, and I did not know
who to thank. I was notified in late November that I
would be shipped out at the end of the month.

Of course, I owed so much to dear Mother, and keeping her informed was always a priority.

Dearest Mother:

*I've just finished my paper work and have everything
in order. My new assignment is at Lackland AFB in San
Antonio. I took the Oath of Commissioned Officer
yesterday, and was the only female (surrounded by
nineteen men) to pledge allegiance to my country and to
our government. I had goose bumps up and down my
spine as I stood there, my right hand raised, and repeated
the Oath of Office. For the very first time, I realized and
understood that I had been accepted to duty with our
United States Air Force!*

I swallowed a big lump in my throat and breathed a silent prayer that God would give me the strength and courage to perform all duties assigned. Since I fear nothing, not even Fear, I am ready, willing and able to serve honorably.

The news from Asia isn't good. This sudden turn of events is not a surprise, and unfortunately, is exactly what I expected. Although I am far from being a military strategist, I think we shall be forced to withdraw from Korea. Such action might be the advent of World War III.

Once I get myself settled at Lackland, I am going to get another Cocker Spaniel—I need someone to talk to, and someone who understands.

Your loving daughter,
Hazel Jane

It is December 24, 1950, and I'm settled in Lowry AFB in Denver, Colorado. Tonight a few of us are celebrating Christmas Eve, so I can now catch my breath and review my situation.

I came here from Lackland AFB with a group of women who had just finished basic training. It is exactly what I wanted. The women will receive more advanced training, then join a WAF Training Squadron. As Adjutant of the Squadron, I'm responsible for everything except their classroom training.

Their Squadron Commander is Captain Watt. My official title is Adjutant of the 3429th WAF Student Squadron. Being responsible for the welfare of several hundred women is no small task. I have already had to fly to Cheyenne, Wyoming to resolve a sticky personal issue involving two of the girls.

Since I must be away from home for Christmas, Captain Watt and her mother have invited me over for Christmas dinner tomorrow. I am happy to have such a friendly relationship and I do appreciate their kindness. It's always hard to spend Christmas without your family, but this will be the next best thing.

Captain Watt is a Chicago native, short and wiry with light brown hair. She takes her position quite seriously and can act very stern when necessary. She also has a wry sense of humor that makes her easy to talk to. When I visited her home once before, she played LPs of her favorite big bands. We even danced a little jitterbug together, with her mother clapping cheerfully to encourage us.

We'll attend Christmas Mass together tomorrow morning. Since my time in Brazil, I understand and respect the rituals of the Catholic mass, and I look forward to joining them at the service. Of course, I would prefer celebrating the birth of Jesus with my family in Macon at my Vineville United Methodist Church. I'll do my best to make sure we'll all be together next year.

THIRTY-TWO

I t's time to admit the obvious: I've turned into a "desk pilot". While still hoping to take to the air, I'm too new to military life in the United States Air Force to rock the boat. My commanding officer has been kind and patient with me as I learn the "Air Force way".

I tell everyone I'm completely happy at work. But in my journal, I need to be honest. I am grateful that they gave me the opportunity to re-enter the aviation world. I'm pleased that Major Watt and I get along so well. She sees my potential and has taught me a lot in four short months.

But "flying a desk" is not where I want to end up. Soon I hope to be adding to the over 6,000 flying hours I've logged so far.

My mother was so thrilled to receive a very thoughtful letter from my commanding officer that she sent it on to me.

3429th Student Squadron, 3415th Technical Training Group
Lowry Air Force Base, Denver, Colorado
Mrs. Bessie P. Raines,
Massee Apartments, College Street, Macon, Georgia
5 March 1951

Dear Mrs. Raines:
   Hazel has been here at Lowry with the WAF
Squadron since 20 December 1950, and it occurred to me

*that you might like to hear a little bit about the fine job
she has been doing.*

*When Hazel reported in and was assigned as
Adjutant, I am sure that you, as well as she, wondered
how she would like "flying a desk". She has probably told
you that during my absence on leave in January the acting
commanding officer received her orders for transfer and as
a result, Hazel was catapulted into being Commanding
Officer, Adjutant and supply officer, all at one time. Her
handling of a difficult situation certainly reflected her fine
previous training. Upon my return, I found everything in
calm good order.*

*In other words, Mrs. Raines, Hazel is successfully
qualifying as a competent "desk pilot" with far less "flying
time" than that which made her skilled in her former
field. Her adjustment has been remarkable, both as to
attitude and approach to the tasks to be done. She has
gained the admiration and respect of the "old timers"
among our enlisted personnel—quite an accomplishment
in itself.*

*As her mother you must always have been extremely
proud of her. This is being written to add to that pride.*

*We are all looking forward to the time when you will
visit us here.*

*Sincerely yours,
Marion L. Watt Major,
USAF Commanding*

Mother hand-wrote Major Watt a heartfelt response and
sent me a copy. Her tender sentiments brought me to tears,

especially when she mentioned how proud she was of me. I am also very proud of her!

She wrote Major Watt that she knew I was pursuing what I most liked in life and was completely happy. How could I disagree with her? I hope and pray that I'm just passing a short time here until my next opportunity. Please Lord, may it be in the skies.

It's May of 1952. I'm working as a recruiter in Tampa, Florida. My Station Commander is Major Fritz, Air Force, and my title is Assistant Station Commander in Charge. We have twenty-one enlisted people and five civilians here in the Tampa Office.

Major Fritz will retire next month, and I'm in line to become Tampa District Commander. As Direct Supervisor of female recruiting, I will spend half my time away from Tampa, supervising and assisting recruiters in the seventeen counties.

My staff car is a four-door Chevrolet—the olive green Army type. I'm leaving tomorrow for a five-day trip in Florida, including stops in St. Petersburg and Sarasota, two cities I really love.

I've recently rented an apartment and am excited about the move. It's in a new four-unit building. I really like the nice big living room, bedroom, tile bath and shower, and small kitchen with a modern electric stove and refrigerator.

I attend *WAC/WAF Recruiters Conferences* in various cities, with a recruiting Sergeant who does most of the driving. We acquaint the public, especially the parents of young girls who might join the Service, with what the Army and Air Force are doing now.

Am I lonely? My mother and sisters, and even my nieces, ask me that. Crum and my other good friends phone me sometimes and ask me too. I've adjusted to my single status, but sometimes wish there was someone in my life to share the joys and sorrows. My sisters write about my sweet nieces, Fabia, Regina and Jeaneane, who are traveling now and loving it. I'm delighted they've shared with me their curiosity about life. Being their Auntie fills a gap in my heart and life that fate took away.

I also miss my beloved Scottie and the cocker spaniels. But when I accepted Jackie's offer for work in Texas, I knew it was best to leave them behind in the loving care of Mrs. Porter. In fact, hers was the only home they had ever known.

Donald—the one man I shared my heart with— phoned me a few months ago to say he's getting married to a woman he went to college with. He told me he was doing well and was content, and he hoped I was too. I am happy for him, but just a little bit sad for me.

When I knew him in Brazil, we agreed our relationship would not be permanent. Yet my heart preserved a crumb of hope that we might pick up where we left off once back in the U.S. We continued to write and talk once in a while, but distance and our businesses undermined our bond. I do wish him the best, and know he wants me to find happiness as well. I want that too.

Personal relationships are so different from the professional and platonic connections that fill my life. I know what to expect when I make a mistake in the cockpit or say the wrong thing to a commanding officer. But the consequences aren't cut and dried in a romance, especially for someone who had never experienced one before.

There's so much trial and error with romance, and it always happens while we're in the middle of a million other things.

It's kind of like getting a flat tire as I'm about to take off, then wondering if I could change the tire without coming to a complete stop. Of course that isn't possible, and luckily my ground crew is prepared to take care of it while I stay buckled up.

In a romance, there's nobody there to help, explain or coach me. I'm on my own and rolling ahead, with no idea of what I might have done wrong or could have done better. So maybe I'll stop daydreaming about love and focus on what I'm good at.

Meanwhile, I'll keep on searching and staying strong, as Daddy always told me.

THIRTY-THREE

In the fall of 1952, I moved to Montgomery, Alabama. Just like in Tampa, I organize "Get Acquainted" Rallies, help my team in recruiting, etc. Here's an example of a familiar activity.

Last week I called on a family in a little town about thirty miles from Montgomery. An eighteen-year-old girl wants to join the Air Force, but her parents are against the idea. She attended university for a year and cannot afford to return, so she's working in a downtown department store.

She's very smart and ambitious and had filled out an application for Officers' Candidate School. When I told her parents she could continue her college education while on duty in the Air Force, they were surprised. Then I explained that after she became an Officer and a leader in military and civilian life, they would be very proud of her and of what she was doing for others.

Today she phoned me to say they had agreed to let her enlist. It inspires me to know that only the most qualified young women are being accepted by various branches of the services. These success stories make my job meaningful to me and my team. Happily, I've had several of them in recent months.

I've just written to Mother and shared my loyalty to our country.

> *I wish you could have been here in Montgomery with me today. Three recently enlisted women and I marched just behind the Color Guard and led the parade from the State Capitol building through town for about a mile. It was quite warm and exhausting, yet I enjoyed every step of the way. With Old Glory in front of me and the Maxwell Air Force Band directly behind playing familiar march music, I stepped out smartly with pride and a prayer of thanks to God that I am American with the unique privilege and pleasure of wearing the uniform of the United States Air Force.*

Once again, I'm attending "school." This one is Adjutant General School at Fort Benjamin Harrison in Indianapolis, Indiana. I drove here, and it was a heck of a drive. The ice and snow were rough, but my Colorado experience in driving through this stuff was so helpful. I'm the only female in this class of two hundred men.

It's interesting to be at an Army Post where 99% of the students are Army. The reason I'm here is because I'm "on loan to the Army". We'll be going to school six days a week, and the course is very interesting so far. Our first exam is next Monday, and we begin our practical work in Public Speaking on Tuesday. For the rest of the week, we will write and present daily speeches.

Our classes are smaller—only thirty-six people in mine. There are five other Officers, twenty-nine enlisted men and one enlisted woman. Soon they will separate us from enlisted people because of our more advanced subject courses. I know I'm going to be working like crazy, and can soon add another diploma to my collection.

I've just finished the courses. Graduation from TAG (The Adjutant General School) was impressive. The Chaplain opened and closed the ceremony with a prayer. A full Colonel—the Commanding Officer of the School—gave the address. We marched up, saluted and were presented with our diplomas. And now, I'm returning to Montgomery, Alabama. It's going to be swell to be comfortable again in good weather. I could handle the cold at Fort Ben, but not the dampness.

I was hardly back in Alabama when I heard about my new orders: a transfer to Omaha, Nebraska. I was already packing my boxes to move there in late September of 1953, when I learned that wasn't going to happen.

"Lt. Raines, let me congratulate you on your new position and post. The Captain of Travis Air Force Base (a few miles from San Francisco) requests your presence as the next Squadron Commander, effective immediately. He is retiring, and he's chosen you."

That was quite a sudden and welcome change in plans! Travis Squadron has only one hundred women—about one-fourth the size of my Squadron at Lowry.

Officers are classified in a specialty field, and mine is personnel and administrative work. Because of that, I head the list for "those most wanted for an overseas assignment." They asked me if I were interested in an assignment in England, and I told them "Not right now, thank you."

I'm trying to make my promotion to Captain, and my paperwork for that will move forward next week. Soon I'll turn thirty-eight, and I find that I enjoy working with these younger women, who call me "Mother". I'm WAF Staff Advisor for all enlisted personnel "on matters such as marriage, unsuitable career assignments, health and personal matters".

The most wonderful news reached me at the end of May. Jackie Cochran phoned me here at Travis. I wasn't in so my assistant took the message, and she was so excited to speak with Jackie Cochran. I later learned that my mother gave Jackie my new number, after a nice chat.

When I phoned Jackie back, she answered immediately.

"Oh Hazel, it's so good to hear your voice," she began cheerfully. "Are you well?"

I laughed. "No major health problems to speak of," I told her. "And I really like it here. How about you?"

"I'm healthy and happy. You may remember I told you in our last phone call that I wanted to challenge the world speed record for women, then held by Jacqueline Auriol."

"And did you?" I asked.

"Indeed I did, with a borrowed plane from the Air Vice-Marshal of the Royal Canadian Air Force. The U.S. Air Force refused to lend me one of theirs."

"So what happened, Jackie?"

"I managed to set a new 100 mile speed record of 652.5 mph on May 18, 1953!"

I was speechless. I felt so proud of her, and honored that she'd share this news with me.

"Congratulations, my friend. What's next?" I asked.

She laughed out loud. "You didn't let me finish. There's more."

She told me that during the course of that run, the Sabre she was flying went supersonic, and Jackie Cochran became the first woman to break the sound barrier!

"You are amazing, Jackie. You must know how proud we all are of you! I'll get the word out, but the others I flew with probably already know. I'm a little slower in keeping up with current aviation events."

"My dear, I was sure you would let the others know. I can always count on you. Anyway, I wanted to know how you are."

It was my turn to laugh. "Well Jackie, I guess we can now say, 'The sky's the limit' and mean it."

"See you in the air, Hazel. Be well."

THIRTY-FOUR

My roommate Poole and I drove 135 miles to Travis Lodge last weekend. This Lodge is owned by the Base. We arrived at noon, and discovered it was snowed in. That meant we had to park about a mile from the Lodge and walk the rest of the way, carrying boots, jackets, a weekend kit, etc. The snow was so soft we kept sinking in half way to our knees. When we arrived, we collapsed into the sofa by the big fireplace and gulped hot coffee.

After lunch, we hiked to the Ski Lodge, sat on the sunny veranda and watched skiers racing down the expert slope for a while. Then we took a cable car to the highway. This was down a steep hill, over a train shed and down a 30-foot ladder.

The next day I woke up early to start my survey work for a new Scouting program. After breakfast Poole and I retraced our steps to the Ski Lodge, about 7,000 feet above sea level. Then we rode the chair lift up to the summit, where the ski run begins. I forgot to apply any protection from the sun, which reflected intensely off the snow. After two hours on the top, as we descended on the chair lift, my face started to feel like it was on fire.

After I plastered thick sunburn lotion on my face we hiked back to my car and finally reached Travis about six o'clock. Poole anxiously watched my forehead swell and puff out like a soufflé. She took me to the hospital, where a doctor said I had second degree burns and gave me pills.

I kept cold compresses on my head all day Monday, with a wad of cold gauze over one eye and then the other as I worked from home. I could feel fluid in my forehead moving slowly down to my eyes. They remained partially closed all day Monday, Tuesday and Wednesday, when it finally went away.

Now my entire face is as red as a beet and peeling. The oddest part is that there's no pain. I faced a lot of teasing from the people at Headquarters about "my new look".

After nearly thirteen years, I'll be working in Jolly Ol' England again, as Adjutant to the 11th Communication Squadron of the Third Air Force. But first I'll spend a few days at Camp Kilmer, New Jersey, processing paperwork, then the weekend off to shop and play in New York City, including attending some radio and television shows. Wearing my uniform, I know I'll have no trouble getting tickets.

Last night I was sitting in the Officers' Lounge when a Lieutenant asked if I knew where she could find Hazel Raines. She looked familiar, and I asked her why she needed to find Hazel Raines.

"We were in training together at Sweetwater, Texas when I was a WASP." She answered, coming a step closer. She squinted, and grinned. "Hazel? Is that you?"

She pointed to the scar on my head from my recent burns. "You can't fool me; you're up to your old tricks."

After some warm laughter and a big hug, Virginia Sweat

and I settled down to "catch up". We were delighted to realize we both have the same assignment for England, and that we're shipping out together. What wonderful luck! We will have a great time together.

Virginia has decided to ship her '51 Chevrolet to England, which gave us a great excuse to go into the city and arrange this. And, naturally we'll do some shopping as well.

We enjoyed the weekend in New York City, saw some television shows and even went to the theater. The next day we rested for our upcoming trip across the Pond.

This will be so different from our first arrival in England, after having sailed from Nova Scotia, Canada in a fruit boat for twenty-seven days. This time we'll fly the Southern route in a four-engine C-54.

Now it is several days later, and we've arrived in England. It was indeed a comfortable flight—smooth all the way and with excellent weather. The ship was as plush as any commercial airplane. We flew at 17,000 feet all the way and landed at Lajes Air Force Base in the Azores at 7:00 p.m. During the flight to Scotland I slept the entire trip.

The Third Air Force is in South Ruislip, just outside London. I believe I'll live in London—not on the Base—so I plan to spend a week there getting settled and finding a place to live.

My squadron is 90% male—10% WAF enlisted personnel. This will be my first time serving as an Officer in a male Squadron. It should be quite interesting. In a few days I'm traveling to Norway. After two days in Germany, it will be on to Paris for a week, and finally, Sweden in the middle of October.

I've been too busy to contact my dear friends and former hosts in Maidenhead, the Littlehales. I'm excited to see them soon. We've been friends for thirteen years now, and have never lost contact through all my moves. I will be sure to see them—perhaps in early October.

Hotel Metropole, Lisbon, Portugal
Friday Evening, 8 October 1954

Dearest Mother:

We had a wonderful flight today from London to Lisbon. We left London, or rather Ruislip, which is where I'm stationed, at 0900 hours and landed here just five hours later. We made the trip in the General's plane so it was quite a luxurious jaunt. Ten minutes after we took off, I was stretched out in my compartment sound asleep. The pilot awakened me at noon for a sandwich and from there on until landing, I sat up and looked out the window, wishing I was rated to fly this kind of passenger craft.

I'm excited to be in Portugal and practice my language skills again. I will study French while I'm in England, which I can use in France.

Tonight in Lisbon, I'm on the balcony, overlooking the Avenida de Republica, the heart of Lisboa. If I didn't know better, I would say I'm back in Brazil! The language is coming back easily, and I've managed several conversations already in Portuguese. After about a half day's work tomorrow, I plan to "sight- see" all afternoon.

We fly to Greece on Sunday. I'll be in Athens one day, then to Rome, Italy for a day and back to England on Wednesday. I wish I could explain what I'm doing, but I cannot. Remember when I ferried in England and couldn't give you details about my work? It's the same situation now. I think one day I'll write a book. Of course, you would probably be the only person who would read it; but you have always been my best supporter.

Travel is a wonderful educational experience. Maybe what has happened to me is a supplement for what could have been.

I am watching people in the square below dashing about, going where for what and why; they don't know, nor do I. Perhaps in our Democratic world of today, they are in a hurry to discover an answer to a simple and peaceful way of life. Is that in our stars?

Please give my love to all,
Hazel Jane

THIRTY-FIVE

I moved from the hotel to a house, just ten minutes from the Base. It has a large, clean bedroom with a small kitchen. The homeowners are my age, without children, and have fixed up this semi-apartment to rent to American visitors. Mr. and Mrs. Allen work in London for Greek Air Lines. He's an ex-RAF pilot; she's Greek and has lived in London for six years. They furnish linens, dishes, and utilities, etc. The rent is about half of what I was paying at the hotel. They have a television set and radio, a cat and a dog, a garden, and a garage for my car when I get it.

The Littlehales wrote a very nice letter and invited me to come down for Thanksgiving. I also received an invitation for the week before Thanksgiving from my friend Phil and her husband in Bournemouth. She was the Met Officer at Hamble when I was stationed down there.

I ordered a custom-made *Consul* automobile one month ago. The dealer called the factory near London and they started building my *Consul*. All cars are made to order; they do not carry stock on the floor. I stipulated how I wanted it built and what accessories I wanted. They have only a basic plan for the auto, and each buyer specifies the interior and exterior design. I've gotten a bang out of "designing" my own car. It will be light blue with blue leather seats! I ordered a heater, but not a radio. It goes about 35 miles on a gallon of petrol.

Tomorrow I'm driving to London to get my driver's license, then next week to Bournemouth to spend the holiday with Phil, her husband and their baby. The following week, I'm off to Germany, where I hope to pick up some Christmas gifts for my family.

I've registered to take Business Law and French classes on the Base. I'll receive four college credits for my Law course and three for the French classes. I'm writing my sisters that one day I'll be educated—one way or another.

I have quite a big job between now and Christmas: planning a Christmas party for fifty-three orphans living in a Catholic home. The children are between five and seventeen, and I need to find appropriate gifts for all of them. I'm borrowing a movie to show that day and I'll decorate a large Christmas tree with the help of a few friends. The First Sergeant, who weighs about 240 pounds, is looking forward to being our Santa Clause.

My new car did very well on the drive to Bournemouth, which is only 100 miles away. I drove slowly because I had only 300 miles on this car. The auto rules are very different here. I can't drive over 40 miles per hour until I've logged 1,000 miles on the odometer. This car is a four cylinder, 45 horse power English Ford, considered a big auto over here. It's a right-hand drive, something I had to get used to. It's perfect for me, since I love learning new things.

My friends Phil and her husband Denis were wonderful hosts last weekend. They have a seven-month-old baby boy, Joshua, who is adorable and fun to play with. Phil and I sat up until two a.m. looking at photos and asking each other over and over again, "Remember this—remember that?"

"Oh Hazel, look at this photo of us!" she exclaimed. "Don't we look so young?"

I grinned. "You look the same, Phil. I've gained some weight since then."

"And Jackie…how lovely she looks. I wonder if she's aged at all."

I told her about our recent phone call, and she said she felt equally proud. Neither one of us had any idea that she was so "disliked" in the aviation world.

"It's got to be pure jealousy," I said. "And she does have a strong personality. I think it intimidates people, but it's how she has accomplished so much."

Phil turned to me with a curious expression. "But Hazel, Nancy Love and Pauline Gower are also very successful in aviation, yet they are admired."

I frowned. "Jackie herself told me that her bossiness and wealth are strikes against her. I don't think she really needs the approval of others. She knows the girls she taught will stand behind her."

Phil nodded. "That we will," she smiled, getting up to return her son to his crib.

Phil's husband Denis is the perfect English gentleman; he constantly surprises me. He loves to prepare coffee and drinks, and enjoys cooking. He even changes Joshua's diapers. This morning he cooked us an "All American" breakfast! After breakfast on Saturday, he disappeared. Soon he was back, wet and dirty. He washed my car, polished the chrome and covered it with a coat of wax. He noticed the dampness was rusting the chrome a little, so he also cleaned that up for me.

Phil is a fortunate woman, and I enjoyed such a fun and relaxing time with them. They've invited me for Christmas and I agreed, on the condition that I would bring and cook the turkey.

Thanksgiving Day turned out to be a lot of fun. My plans with the Littlehales were put on hold when they were suddenly called away, so I took the Tube to London Thursday morning and met three American friends from the Base. We spent the day looking and wishing—the clothes in London are beautiful but very *dear*—British for expensive. No one bought a thing, but we all enjoyed window shopping. We walked over to the American Embassy and celebrated our typical Thanksgiving with our fellow countrymen. On American holidays, the Embassy offers special meals to Americans on duty in England.

My latest trip was to Wiesbaden, Germany. I can honestly say I've never eaten so much. German cooking is out of this world, and without even knowing what I was ordering half the time, I loved it all! My sister Frankie would go mad here with all the choices. It's hard to get along in any foreign country unless you know the language or have someone to interpret it. My German and French are improving, but people say I talk with a "Southern accent". Imagine that!

Germans in West Germany are very friendly and courteous and seem to be taking to our American ideas and ideals without resentment. Their recovery from the war is unbelievable, both economically and socially. The new government is making remarkable strides in what we hope is the right direction.

What a small world it is! I saw seven people I knew in Wiesbaden and Paris. To top it off, I ran into a WAF Officer in Wiesbaden who had been with me at Sweetwater in 1943. Next I ran into a Major I taught to fly at Fort Lauderdale. He took me out for dinner and to a German night club last Friday night, and we had a great time reminiscing. I'm amazed at how quickly time flies over here.

THIRTY-SIX

Wednesday Night, 8 December, 1954

Dearest Mother,

I was happy to receive a letter from you today and also the fruit cake you sent. I haven't opened the package yet because I want to wait for Christmas.

I have a new title: WAF Advisor, or Assistant Chief of Staff Personnel. I basically do the same work but receive more money. I will now accompany all WAF enlisted personnel on trips to France and Germany for athletic tournaments (softball, basketball, bowling etc.). I know this will be fun for me and team-building for all of us.

I enjoyed working with the 11th Communications, but much prefer working with the WAF. Now I'll be planning another Christmas party for over one-hundred WAFs. I'll still help out with the orphans, but that is pretty much in place and the Lieutenant who replaced me will handle that.

Oh Mother, once again I'm moving. This seems to be the new theme of my life: changing jobs and houses frequently. I hate to leave the home where I'm living now, but the heating there isn't adequate and we seem to run out of hot water for bathing about twice a week. I've found a flat just a mile from Base. It's small with one bedroom, a living room with a couch that can be made

into a bed, a kitchen and my own bath. The living room
has a gas heater, and I'll buy an Aladdin oil burner for the
bedroom, and a small electric heater for the bath. I'll
move next weekend, on the 18th. I'm excited to get my
own place where I can invite friends to come for a meal, a
game of cards, or even to spend a week, if you or the
family were to visit!

I should close now and get back to preparations for
Christmas.

Your loving Hazel

Christmas has come and gone. As usual, some of my plans changed at the last minute. I had to cancel my trip to Bournemouth to see Phil and her family, so I could be with the girls in the Squadron on Christmas morning. It's hard for them to be away from their families, and I remember that feeling of total despondency and sadness.

On Christmas Eve I learned that one of my girls had been in a car accident and suffered a rather bad head injury. I stayed with her in the hospital while they examined and bandaged her, and until they assured me she would be fine in a few days.

Christmas morning Bobbie (my WAF friend) and I cooked breakfast for fifty WAFs, and then we sat around and sang Christmas carols until noon. We enjoyed ourselves and basked together in the sense of camaraderie. I was glad I chose to stay with them, rather than do what I had planned—spend Christmas with Phil and Denis. They said I was welcome any time.

I bought an eight-pound turkey, which my First Sergeant cooked in the Squadron's galley. We've had turkey every day since, and tonight's turkey dinner will finish it off.

I've been spending most of my time working on the WAF athletic program. Last weekend the basketball team from Wiesbaden, Germany came to play our WAF team. We lost one game and won the other. We're now in second place in the Western Conference! I'll take them to Bremerhaven, Germany next weekend.

On February 3rd, I'm taking the team to Wiesbaden for the USA-FR championship game. If they win, there's a good chance I'll take them to the States for about two weeks, where they would play for the Air Force-wide championship. This is a big "if" but we're working hard and crossing our fingers to be able to go. I'd then make a trip home for a few days, and that's so important to me.

I'm also taking my bowling team to Bremerhaven for four days beginning February 24th. We'll travel by boat to Belgium, then take a train to the competition. I'm supposed to go to Paris this weekend, but don't see how I can with so much traveling scheduled for next month.

I need to take some time off to get my clothes cleaned and finish up other personal matters. This job does require travel for about half of every month, but I don't mind because it gives me a wonderful chance to really see France, Holland, Belgium, Denmark, Norway, Sweden, Germany, Switzerland and Italy. This assignment has turned out to be better than I ever dreamed. Honestly, I'm a very lucky gal.

It's been four months since I've had a chance to do some journaling. I really don't know where the time goes. The hours in a day pass by so quickly—I never have a moment for anything personal, since work seems to consume me. I had hoped to finally go to Maidenhead to visit the Little-hales, or perhaps meet them somewhere for several days. It hasn't happened yet, but it will. They've been very patient with me and my crazy schedule.

I plan to take off some time the weekend of the 4th of July. Since this is a holiday for Americans only, we might take a trip westward toward Bath and Bristol through the Cheddar Gorge (where they make that tasty cheese) and on July 5th, we have tickets to see Danny Kaye. He's been playing in London for the past month, so I went early to buy four tickets and was so lucky to get them. They were not cheap, but we know he'll be worth the cost.

On June 30th, we will have a grand celebration. That day marks our eighth birthday as Women in the Air Force. There will be an open house for everyone at the Service Club, where the Commanding General of the Third Air Force and Alfred Drake, a popular British stage and film star, will cut the cake. After all that, all the "Big Wheels" and "little cogs" like me will inspect the WAF billets. In the evening, a buffet dinner will be served, followed by a dance at the club. This takes heaps of planning and hard work, but what worthwhile project doesn't?

And on July 10th, Colonel Gray, WAF Director from Washington D.C., will visit for four days. With so much to plan for, plus my normal activities, I imagine the next few weeks will fly by before I even realize it. Keeping busy does have its perks.

THIRTY-SEVEN

One of my British friends has the most beautiful Miniature Poodle. She had a litter of seven pups two months ago, and my friend asked me if I would like a male puppy. So Andy is now mine. He's a little white puffy thing and will probably not weigh nine pounds when fully grown. Apparently, he isn't interested in becoming housebroken. My First Sergeant took one of his siblings and has offered to train Andy for me while I'm away. But while I'm here, he stays with me in my office and is a sweet little boy.

Christmas is three months away, and I'm trying to put together a trip to Georgia. I'm scheduled to go to Washington on business around December 15th, and will be busy with that for a few days. But I have permission to leave from Washington on December 22nd and fly to Macon. Unfortunately, I need to be back here on January 1st. That leaves very little time to celebrate the holidays with my family. On the other hand, it works out expense-wise. I get Military airfare rates (about 40% discounted) so I should just jump at the chance and go.

My family will be surprised to see that my hair is turning grey. It doesn't show much because it's naturally a light color, but I still cover it up with a rinse. I have a very good beautician at the Base.

It seems odd to me that the older I get, the more I miss my family. Is that because my life is so busy and often hectic, and my family gives me peace? Or, is it because I'm a Georgia gal and have not lived anywhere that even vaguely resembles my life there? I find myself becoming melancholy. Maybe it's from being middle-aged. Whatever the reason, it just feels very important to be with them now.

I was able to spend an extra week in Macon, and had a fun time with friends and family members! I needed the comfort of returning to my roots, and comfort I got! The Southern food was amazing, especially the fried chicken. One thing never changes—the people. I am so proud to be a Southerner, surrounded by loving, caring, respectful people. And we really do wear cheerful smiles and send good wishes to each other for "a good year, journey, life," etc. I'm carrying some beautiful memories in my heart.

I credit my natural ability to fit in and turn strangers into generous collaborators with my Southern upbringing. There's obviously a big difference between a small Georgia city and a highly mechanized military base. Yet I wonder if my life in the hospitable community of Macon may have shown me how people from different backgrounds can comfortably connect and help each other, as long as everyone likes to see the others smile.

This brings up some happy memories of my good friend from high school named Eleanor. She was born into one of Macon's "old" families. Her grandparents had been quite wealthy, and had two live-in employees. Eleanor's parents weren't wealthy, but felt responsible for Suzi and Cleveland as they grew older, so they continued living and working in Eleanor's home.

When I visited Eleanor, she was often in the kitchen with Suzi, laughing and sharing stories. Suzi seemed like another mother to me too, teaching us traditional songs as she cooked dinner or polished the family's old "coin" silverware. Our differences just disappeared in laughter.

My parents taught us to treat everyone with respect and consideration. Seeing Eleanor and Suzi acting like family reminded me that people should always be respectful to each other. I have tried to follow their example as a team member or officer in the WAFs. Maybe that's why I never felt any awkward desire to show my importance to others. I hope this made me easier to work with as a leader. Memories of happily singing spirituals in the kitchen with Eleanor and Suzi still bring me a special joyful feeling.

On a recent subway trip in New York City, I was surprised by the lack of contact between strangers traveling together. Even leaning against each other, they avoided any eye contact—especially with anyone from another race or heritage. Suddenly, I was overwhelmed with feeling. I missed Georgia and blinked back tears as I pulled out my silver coin. I could see my Daddy's face as he presented it to me. I gave God thanks for allowing me to grow up there.

I had a difficult time getting back to Jolly Ol' England. Bad weather conditions, plus the terrible London fog, delayed my return flight so I had to change planes in New York. Pan American Airlines flew me safely back, and now I have jet lag once again.

I don't know why, but I have been very tired lately. Perhaps my WAF Advisor position and eighteen months of traveling so often have taken a toll. I'm considering requesting a re-assignment, but don't know where I want to be or even in what work capacity. I'm often plagued by confusing ideas about my future, and that's been disconcerting and wearisome.

There's another odd thing happening to me: my back is starting to give me trouble. I haven't had back problems for the last few years, and now they've returned. I talked to my doctor at the Base, and he suggested I see a specialist in Wiesbaden, Germany. I have an appointment and will fly there next month to see what the outcome is. If they decide I need some treatment that can't be done here in England, I'll insist they send me back to the States.

My sister Frankie and her girls are in Paris, having a wonderful time. I told them at Christmas that Paris is my least favorite European city. In personal experiences I've found that the French try to take an American for every penny they can. And prices are so high. Germany is different; Germans are nice to you and don't try to rob you when you go shopping. But my family hasn't experienced what I did, and I'm happy for them. I believe I'll give Mother a call this afternoon; it's quite expensive, but I really miss her.

A month has passed since my last sentence, and I'm feeling much better now, even though I'm back in the hospital for a routine check-up. When we reach the age of forty, we are given a variety of tests, which means we have to be in the hospital for several days. My back problems are lessening, and I'm continuing rehabilitation through medication and physical therapy, including underwater treatments, which I really enjoy.

I was just reminiscing about the trouble I used to have passing a physical exam, due to the extra beat in my heart. Of course they found that same situation here, and they are stumped by it, but the doctors have finally determined that my heart is in good condition. Same old story I've heard for years, but I really am feeling okay.

Tomorrow I will check out of the hospital and take a drive over to the East Coast—perhaps Dover—and relax in the sun on the beach with my puppy Andy. I've been given a couple of days off before starting my new assignment: Special Assistant to the Assistant Chief of Staff of Personnel. The great news is that I will get the same pay as before, will have the same status, and will work only from 8:30 to 5:00 Monday through Friday. This is a wonderful offer, and I'm grateful for it.

THIRTY-EIGHT

Sunday, 22 July 1956
Dearest Mother:

What a beautiful day—I've been sitting in the sun but had to come in—it got too hot for me. Let me bring you up to date. I flew over here to Wiesbaden last week and have been doing nothing but resting, eating, and sleeping. I'm in the 7100 USAF Hospital, and they've been giving me the best attention possible. I'm feeling fine, but do not know how long I will be here.

The only things they can find wrong is my old back and leg, but even so—I'm much better since they intensified the underwater treatments.

Yesterday afternoon I had a glorious surprise: Frankie, Reginald, Fabia and Reg just walked into my room without any warning! We were so happy we all shed tears (most of us anyway). It sure was good seeing them! And then they returned last night to visit for another two hours, bringing magazines, flowers and other presents. They entertained me with stories of their European trip. I wish they could have stayed in Wiesbaden longer, but they have a tour this morning and will leave this afternoon.

The sad part of this story is that it seems I won't be back in London while they are there. Maybe I can convince my doctors to release me. I expect to go back to

London soon, but you might continue writing me here,
until I tell you otherwise. Take care of yourself, and give
my love to all.

> *Lots of love always,*
> *Your Hazel Jane*

A few days later I sent a letter to Frankie and her family. I told them the doctor checked my back and leg and found them much better but will do another myelogram. That will happen on Friday, and the procedure is not simple. They will tap my spine, inject a fluid that's a dye substance, and then take x-rays. If there is any damage or trouble within the spine, it will show up there. After they do this I will have to stay on my back for twenty-four hours. By next Monday, I should know something definite.

I asked them not to write Mother about this, because she would only worry. Then I wrote my own letter to Mother, talking about the fun Frankie and family were having in London, and letting her know they were on their way to Scotland. I did *not* tell Mother that I hated not being able to go with them, and show them the Scotland that I love.

When they were here, Fabia told me all about her wedding plans. That will be quite an event, and I wish I could be there. Who knows—I might be able to make it. Oh well—at least I can dream…

Five days later I wrote another letter to Mother.

August 11, 1956
Dearest Mother,

Well, I am still here in the hospital but feeling fine. Thought for sure I would be out by now, but they won't release me until they are sure I am 100% fit for duty. I'm still taking Physical Therapy treatments and they seem to be helping my back and leg quite a bit. I get around much better than I have in a long time; however, the doctor told me yesterday that I might need a brace for a while. And if they decide to make a back brace for me, I will be here another two weeks, since it takes that long to have it made and fitted properly. I won't know for sure until next week. Please don't worry since I'm feeling good and know I'm getting better every day.

I'm afraid this hospital life is making me lazy—all I do is eat, rest and sleep. The hospital movie room is down on the first floor and now that I can get around pretty well, I've been going down every night for the past week. It gives me something to do, and I can get away from sick people for a couple of hours.

Lots of love always,
Hazel Jane

I was so happy to finally be released and return to Ruislip, England. I wrote Mother immediately, but she had already learned about it before my letter reached her. The Third Air Force was kind enough to write her and let her know that I was back. Here is the letter she received from the Third Air Force.

Hazel had been hospitalized here at South Ruislip on 5 June 1956 for a recurrence of an old back injury. On July 10th, 1956 she was transferred to the 7100 USAF Hospital in Germany for further neurological examinations and treatment. Subsequently, she was transferred back here on August 26th and discharged from the hospital on August 31st.

I sent Mother another letter at the end of August, cheerful and optimistic.

Wednesday, 27 August 1956
Dearest Mother,

Just a quick note to let you know I am finally back safe and sound. True, I'm still in the hospital, but they told me today they will most likely discharge me in three or four days. I'll then need about fifteen days' leave to get back on my feet again before I return to full duty. I won't mind that at all since my legs feel rubbery.

It's been a long haul, tiresome at times. But I am feeling just grand and know that all this rest I've had will make me feel like a new person. Tell Frankie I found some mail for them when I went by my flat yesterday before returning to the hospital. I will send it to them soon. Oh, it was so great to spend some time with my pup Andy.

I'm looking forward to returning to my reality. I miss you very much, and have had a lot of time to reflect on many happy memories. Please take care, and give my love to all the family.

Lots of love always,
Your Hazel Jane

THIRTY-NINE

Western Union

1956 Sep 20
Mrs. Bessie P Raines
Massee Apts
College Street

REMAINS OF YOUR DAUGHTER, THE LATE 1st LT HAZEL J. RAINES, ARE BEING CONSIGNED TO HART MORTUARY, CHEERY STREET, MACON, GEORGIA DEPARTING VIA RAIL DOVER, DELAWARE 6:26 P.M. 20 SEPT 56. ESCORTED BY CAPTAIN ANNE M. GREGG, REMAINS DUE TO ARRIVE MACON 8:05 P.M. 21 SEPT. 56 ON C OF GEORGIA TRAIN NR 108. MY DEEPEST SYMPATHIES ARE EXTENDED TO YOU AND MEMBERS OF THE DECEDENTS FAMILY.

COMMANDER DOVER AFB DELAWARE

FORTY

Hazel Raines died from health complications on September 4th, 1956. She was forty years old. She had been released from the hospital in England on August 31st.

Hazel had come a long way since her barnstorming days in the 1930s, and had proved herself in ways few women would have dared or even wanted to try in the 1940s. Her legacy to women in aviation, and her role as "Georgia's Pioneer Lady of Flight", merited a posthumous award. She was one of three women honored by the *Georgia Women of Achievement* in 1995.

Memories from her friends portray a modest yet determined young woman, who was considered "a sport". In 1939, "she was seen racing against experienced pilots, accepting defeat with a smile and extending congratulations to the winners".

Each time she returned to Macon, the entire family gathered to celebrate. There was always music, for Hazel played the piano by ear and "could get music out of anything", including the bugle, saxophone, cornet, drums and harmonica. Hazel claimed "she could hear music from the wind whistling through the struts of the wings of an airplane".

When Hazel arrived at Avenger Field to join the WASPs, she seldom discussed her experiences as a ferry pilot. According to a fellow WASP, Peggy Parker Eccles, Hazel did not brag. She was, however, exempted from cross-country flying because of her extensive experience. Her reputation as an excellent pilot followed her there. Peggy remembers that Hazel "was never at a loss as to what to do, had a good sense of humor, liked people, was good company, and had a deep Southern accent".

Hazel had her self-doubts, revealed in some letters to her mother. She may have felt certain personal options were taken away from her at an early age, having had an ovary removed at the age of twenty-two. While the medical practices of the 1930s and 1940s would be highly questioned in the present times, they worked to Hazel's advantage in some ways. Hazel's irregular heartbeat and obvious bouts of asthma would not be tolerated in the world of aviation today. Only her determination to fly and insistent conversations with doctors in several countries kept her in the air.

One request to her mother, written years ago, didn't happen as she expected. *Mother, if you ever get a message that I've been in a crackup and have been killed, don't grieve for me more than you can possibly help; just know I died the way I wanted to.* Hazel did live a life that fulfilled her dreams. And she did it her way.

EPILOGUE

Hazel's mother spoke very little to family members about her daughter after she died in 1956. The grandchildren felt it was just too painful for Bessie. Others believed she did not want to share Hazel's life with the public. Family members simply spoke about Hazel's death as being from a heart attack.

Hazel Jane Raines left a huge legacy to women in aviation. She was the first female reserve pilot called to active duty in 1950. She became a test pilot during her WASP period and relished this work. *"Georgia's Pioneer Lady of Flight"* was honored with several posthumous awards. She was one of three women recognized in 1995 as a *Georgia Women of Achievement* and was inducted into the *Georgia Aviation Hall of Fame.*

Hazel made a lasting impression on everyone who knew her. She was a true pioneer known for her ability to prevail in difficult situations. Seldom complaining or explaining, she constantly honed her technical and people skills by accepting every mistake or oversight as another opportunity to learn and grow.

Once during pilot training, a classmate jokingly commented on Hazel's habit of laughing to herself when she was alone.

Hazel grinned. "I'm not really crazy," she explained. "That's just how I keep from getting upset with myself about mistakes or regrets. It reminds me I can do better next time. It's a habit I picked up from my Daddy."

One student said she taught him to solo in just eight hours. He remembered that Hazel always carried an empty Coke bottle on their flights. He would climb into the front of the Taylor craft while Hazel sat in the rear. One day he asked her, "Why do you have that empty bottle?"

Hazel replied with a grin, "If you freeze and refuse to relinquish the controls, I might have to knock you out." That was typical of her friendly and down-to-earth teaching style.

Hers was a life shaped by bravery, intelligence and charm, as well as the political and social challenges of the day. Her love of friends and family would always be remembered by anyone fortunate enough to know her.

AFTERWORD

"Your limits are somewhere up there, waiting for you to reach beyond infinity."

—Gen. Henry H. "Hap" Arnold

The WASPs eventually flew every aircraft operated by the Army Air Corps, proving that a woman's hand could guide a fighter plane to a perfect landing as well as any man's. Bills were introduced to Congress to give them military rank, and even with General Arnold's support, all efforts to absorb the organization into the military failed.

The women of the WASP fulfilled all expectations of those who initiated the program. In total, they flew over 60 million miles in operational flights in every type of aircraft flown. Thirty-eight WASPs sacrificed their lives in the service of their country during World War II.

On December 20, 1944, the WASP program was deactivated, and pilots were told they were no longer needed. They returned to civilian life with no Veterans' benefits. Then in 1949, the Air Force offered commissions to all former WASPs. One hundred-fifteen women accepted, and twenty-five of them became career officers. Unfortunately, though their commissions were based on their service as WASPs, they never again flew military aircraft.

Finally, in March of 1979, the Department of the Air Force announced that WASP duty qualified as active military service and would include Veterans' benefits. At a 1986 reunion in Sweetwater, Texas, the names of all

WASPs who had lost their lives during the war were read.

Jackie Cochran, Hazel's mentor and friend, joined the Air Force Reserve in 1948 as its first female pilot. She was promoted to Colonel in 1969, then retired the next year. She received three *Distinguished Flying Cross* awards between 1947 and 1964.

After breaking the sound barrier on May 18, 1953, Jackie continued setting aviation speed, distance and altitude records. At the time of her death in 1980, no other pilot held more aviation records than she.

Jackie Cochran was the first woman to land and take off from an aircraft carrier, the first woman to pilot a bomber across the North Atlantic (1941) and fly a jet aircraft on a transatlantic flight. She was the first woman to make an instrument landing, the only woman ever to be President of the *Fédération Aéronautique International*e (1958-1961), the first woman to fly a fixed-wing jet aircraft across the Atlantic, the first pilot to fly above 20,000 feet (6,096 meters) with an oxygen mask, and the first woman to enter the Bendix Transcontinental Race.

She died on August 9, 1980 in Indio, California and is buried in the Coachella Valley Public Cemetery. *Thermal Airport*, which she regularly utilized, was renamed *Jacqueline Cochran Regional Airport* in her honor.

FROM THE AUTHOR

Thank you for reading the story of Hazel Jane Raines. I hope it has inspired you.

I really enjoy introducing heroines like Hazel to open-minded readers. In each of my historical novels, I write about intriguing characters who overcame surprising constraints and challenges. Because of their strength, talents, and skills, these role models demonstrate how perseverance and dedication help "ordinary" people excel at what truly matters to them.

Remember, the sky isn't your limit. What limits us is our dedication to excellence.

Like other people, you've probably wondered what you can offer the world. Which of your goals are most important? How can you achieve them? Hazel, Jackie Cochran, and many other female pilots of that time had to overcome serious prejudice, resentment, and other obstacles.

Every book I've written poses a serious question that few people had asked. For Hazel and her colleagues, it was "Are women physically and mentally capable of piloting huge aircraft during wartime?" Their answer: a resounding "YES!"

Hazel and her fellow female pilots refused to accept limiting answers. Hazel's story reveals how she and others overcame their constraints and doubts. The sky is never the limit for someone who believes in herself.

QUESTIONS FOR DISCUSSION

1. This novel spans twenty years and includes letters from almost every year. Did you enjoy learning about Hazel's thoughts and experiences through this approach?

2. All my historical novels touch on the tension between choice and destiny. Which of Hazel's premonitions did you suspect would come to pass? Why?

3. Women are often considered more skillful at forming and sustaining friendships than men. Do you feel Hazel was an exception to this stereotype? Why or why not?

4. At one turning point, Hazel recognized a need for intimacy in her life. How did she define "intimacy" and how did that impact her choices? How is that definition different from today?

5. Did Hazel have epiphanies throughout her life? If so, which ones can you relate to?

6. Throughout her life, Hazel considered her father an important mentor. Who has been your most influential mentor? Who have you mentored?

7. Her relationship with her mother is a continuing thread in this story. How would you characterize it? Did you notice it change or evolve over the years?

8. During her time in Europe, Hazel interacted with some famous people. Which person would you have liked to meet on her list? Who is the most famous person you've ever met? What impressed you most about him or her?

9. Hazel was always ready to try new experiences and walk away from her comfort zone. How do you compare with her?

10. What prompted Hazel's decision to leave Brazil? What had she realized about herself?

11. The characters we care about most are usually those with whom we identify. Could you easily identify with Hazel? With Jackie Cochran? Or with another character?

12. Did Hazel think she was different from her pilot friends? What values or activities affected her sense of camaraderie?

13. Hazel knew exactly what she wanted and spent her life working to reach that goal. Did this enhance her life style, or detract from it?

14. Do you agree that the novel's theme might be that we think we know where we're guiding our lives, but can never be sure what that will look like? Or can you think of a better theme?

15. What do you think of this new (to me) approach to writing an historical novel? The narrative is created around Hazel, but I had to add some events and insert a few people into those events who didn't exist. Would this be another way to reach a wider audience so more people can learn from history?

16. The quest for personal fulfillment for women is explored in my novel. What are your thoughts on how things have and haven't changed for women since the 1940s and 1950s?

RESOURCES

Primary Sources

Hawkins, Regina T, *Pioneer Lady of Flight: Hazel Jane Raines, A Biography in Letters*, Macon, Georgia, Mercer University Press, 1996.

Lomax, Judy, *Women of the Air*, New York, N.Y., Ivy Books, 1986.

Van Wagenen Keil, Sally, T*hose Wonderful Women In Their Flying Machines: The Unknown Heroines of World War II*, New York, N.Y., Four Directions Press, 2000.

Secondary Sources

Carl, Ann B., *A Wasp Among Eagles*, New York, N.Y., Smithsonian Institution, 1999.

Chirhart, Ann Short and Clark, Kathleen Ann, *Hazel Jane Raines (1916-1956): Georgia's First Woman Pilot and her Band of Sisters during WWII*, University of Georgia Press, 2014.

History of the Air Transport Command: *Women Pilots in the Air Transport Command, Historical Branch, Intelligence and Security Division*, Air Transport Command, 1946.

Merryman, Molly, *Clipped Wings-The Rise and Fall of Women Air Force Service Pilots (WASPs) of World War II*. NYU Press, 1998.

O'Connell Pearson, P., *Fly Girls: The Daring American Women Pilots Who Helped Win WWII*, New York, N.Y., Simon & Schuster, 2018.

Schrader, Helena Page, *Sisters in Arms*, South Yorkshire, 5702 A5, United Kingdom, Pen & Sword Books Limited, 1988.

Schrader, Helena Page, *Winged Auxiliaries: Women Pilots in the UK and US during World War II*, United Kingdom, The Royal Institute of Navigation, 2006.

Simbeck, Rob, *Daughter of the Air: The Brief Soaring Life of Cornelia Fort*, New York, N.Y., Grove Press, 1999.

Simpson Smith, Elizabeth, *Women In Aviation*, New York, N.Y., Walker and Company 1981.

Citations, Magazine and Newspaper Articles

Bulman, Morgan, *Five Things to Know About the Spitfire—The Legend of Dunkirk*, Smithsonian National Air and Space Museum, July 21, 2017.

Cochran, Jacqueline, *Final Report on Women Pilot Program*, Army Air Forces Report 6-1262, Headquarters, AAF, 1945.

England, Women Pilots, U.S. Congress, House, Committee on Veterans' Affairs, Select Subcommittee, "Hearing on Granting Veterans' Status to WASPs", 95th Cong. 1st Sess., September 20, 1977.

Girl Pilots, Life Magazine, New York City, N.Y., July 19, 1943.

History of the Air Transport Command: Women Pilots in the Air Transport Command, Historical Branch, Intelligence and Security Division, Air Transport Command, 1946.

Holtzclaw, Mary M., *Georgia Girl in Spitfire Crash*, Atlanta Journal and Constitution, September 8, 1943.

Holtzclaw, Mary M., *Georgia's Flying Lady is the First WASP Recalled by Air Force*, Atlanta Journal and Constitution Magazine, December 17, 1950.

New Biography Tells Story of Wesleyan's Pioneer Lady of Flight, Wesleyan Magazine, Spring of 1997.

Parrish, Nancy, *WASP FAQ*, *Wings Across America*, Nancy@wingsacrossamerica.org.

Scharr, Adela Rick, *Sisters in the Sky, Vol. 1, The WAFS*, Gerald, MO, Patrice Press, 1986.

The Watchtower, Wesleyan College, Macon, Georgia, September 26, 1941.

The Wesleyan Alumnae-Article on Hazel Jane Raines, Wesleyan College, November, 1943.

The Wesleyan Alumnae-Article on Hazel Jane Raines, Wesleyan College, November, 1946.

The Wesleyan Alumnae-Article on Hazel Jane Raines, Wesleyan College, Fall of 1989.

Wesleyan Magazine, *New Biography Tells Story of Wesleyan's Pioneer Lady of Flight*, Spring of 1997.

Internet Articles

www.//airandspace.si.edu/topics/aviation2

www.//airandspace.si.edu/multimedia-gallery//
98-15197hjpg

www.//airforcehistoryindex.org. National Museum of the Mighty Eighth.

www.//americanmuseum.com, National Museum of the Mighty Eighth. WASP Collection.

www.en.wikipedia.org/georgia/aviationhalloffame/
Raines.

https://en.wikipedia.org/wiki/Jackie_Cochran

www.//express.co.uk/news/world/1091040/Rio-Carnival-2019-rio-de-janeiro-carnival-2019. February 22, 2019

www.//findagrave.com/memorial/55983446/hazel-jane-raines: memorial page for Hazel Jane Raines (21 April 1916-4 September 1956), Riverside Cemetery, Macon, Bibb County, GA, U.S.A.

www.//gaaviationhalloffame.com/hall-of-fame/Raines.

www.///galileo.usg.edu/, Georgia Historical Newspaper-Digital Library of Georgia—Georgia's Virtual Library Galileo. *Miss Hazel Raines of Macon to become Instructor in R.A.F.*, March 17, 1941.

www.//georgiaencyclepedia.org/article/education/wesleyan-college. Huff, Christopher Allen, *Wesleyan College*, New Georgia Encyclopedia, University of Georgia Press, May 3, 2017.

www.//georgiawomen.olrg/gwa-hall-of-fame.

www.//georgiahumanities.org/2017/04/13/hazel-raines-paved-the-way-for-generations-of-female-pilots. Hutton, Allison, *Hazel Raines paved the way for Generations of Female Pilots*, Georgia humanities, Georgia Humanities Council.

www.///galileo.usg.edu/, Georgia Historical Newspaper-Digital Library of Georgia—Georgia's Virtual Library Galileo. *Miss Hazel Raines of Macon to become Instructor in R.A.F.*, March 17, 1941.

www.//nationalmuseum.of.mil/visit/museum/exhibits. *Civilian Pilot Training Program*, National Museum of the U.S. Air Force, May 4, 1925.

www.//rio-carnival.net

www.//spitfire-join-the-fighting-html.

ABOUT THE ARTIST

This is Gini Steele's seventh historical novel cover art for author Pamela Bauer Mueller. Combining her love of photography and history, she enjoys the challenge of creating the "perfect" cover image for Pamela's books. Over the years, Gini and her husband Richard created an extensive collection of photographic images of times gone by. Throughout their work with historical societies, archivists and researchers, they realized there was a need to restore and reproduce these images and make them available before they became lost forever.

Gini enjoys the challenge of interpreting the old negatives and photographs in her darkroom. She prints the silver gelatin photographs by hand, one at a time. Once they are printed, she tints them by hand. After the hand-tinting is accomplished, Gini uses digital technology to complete the image, creating a unique piece of art.

Gini has recently moved to James Island, SC with her cat Penelope Butterbeans. She loved her many years residing in Beaufort, SC but will be closer to her family on James Island. Gini can work anywhere there is beauty and nature.